THE THREE DAYS
A Liturgical Guide
Second Edition

by Lawrence J. Johnson

The Federation of Diocesan Liturgical Commissions

Acknowledgements

Scripture texts used in this work are taken from the *Lectionary for Mass for Use in the Dioceses of the United States of America, second typical edition, Volume 1*. Copyright © 1970, 1997, 1998 Confraternity of Christian Doctrine, Inc., Washington, D.C. All rights reserved. No part of this work may be reproduced or transmitted in any form or by any means, electronic or mechanical, including photocopying, recording, or by any information storage and retrieval system, without permission in writing from the copyright owner. The poetic English translation of the sequences of the Roman Missal are taken from the *Roman Missal* approved by the National Conference of Catholic Bishops of the United States © 1964 by the National Catholic Welfare Conference, Inc. All rights reserved. Excerpts from *National Statutes for the Catechumenate* © 1988. United States Catholic Conference, Inc., Washington, D.C. Reprinted with permission. All rights reserved. Excerpts from *Thirty-Five Years of the BCL Newsletter* © 2004, United States Conference of Catholic Bishops, Washington, D.C. Reprinted with permission. All rights reserved.

The English translation of the Psalm Responses from *Lectionary for Mass* © 1969, 1981, 1997, International Commission on English in the Liturgy Corporation (ICEL); excerpts from the English translation of *Documents on the Liturgy, 1963-1979: Conciliar, Papal, and Curial Texts* © 1982, ICEL; excerpts from the English translation of *Rite of Christian Initiation of Adults* © 1985, ICEL; excerpts from the English translation of *The Roman Missal* © 2010, ICEL. Reprinted with permission. All rights reserved.

Excerpts from *"Paschalis sollemnitatis," Circular letter concerning the preparation and celebration of the Easter feasts : January 16, 1988*, Libreria Editrice Vaticana, Vatican City, Office of Publishing and Promotion Services, United States Catholic Conference, Washington, D.C. Reprinted with permission. All rights reserved.

Interior art by Jane Pitz; cover art by Rosemary Moak; cover design by Janna R. Stellwag.

The Three Days: A Liturgical Guide
© 2001, 2012 (Second Edition)
Federation of Diocesan Liturgical Commissions (FDLC)
415 Michigan Avenue, N.E., Suite 70, Washington, D.C. 20017.
Phone: 202-635-6990. Fax: 202-529-2452.
E-mail: publications@fdlc.org. Web page: www.fdlc.org.
All rights reserved.

Preface

As Roman Catholics we are assuredly and unabashedly a ritual people, for when we gather for worship we carry out certain inherited patterns of action, repeated time and time again by the Church down through the ages. As we do so, we are a people of "memory," recalling not only God's past actions but also that divine action which is presently preparing us for the establishment of a kingdom of love and justice; it is the foundation of this kingdom that we, through our worship and our lives, are called to create.

It has been said that the word "worship" is primarily a verb and not a noun. So it is that when we gather, we do things — we use water, wheat, wine, oil, ashes, incense, and even light and darkness to express who we are, what we believe, and what we hope to become. Using texts both old and new, we dialogue, listen, proclaim, speak, and sing. Furthermore, there are times when we are called to remain silent, allowing the Spirit of God to speak within our hearts. Since "doing" requires the use of the body, we impose hands, we uplift hands, we fold hands, we sign with the cross, we stand, sit, kneel, genuflect, and bow.

With its symbols and signs, ritual action allows us to express our very identity as a Church of baptized persons and to enter into communion with the God who is the source of all being.

Those who prepare and lead these rituals are entrusted with traditions that have nourished countless generations of Catholics, traditions demanding respect and care. Although carried out by the members of a local community, the rituals also belong to the wider Church, the so-called Church Universal. The general pattern of the ritual and the individual rites themselves as given to us are to be respected, always carried out with elegance, proper solemnity or simplicity, and the utmost of care. Although there is no place for liturgical tinkering, there is always need for creativity so that the texts and directives contained in the official books may take life, may be enfleshed in a celebration that profoundly engages the hearts and minds of those participating.

As we utilize our resources in preparing the Triduum, we should never forget that our objective is not to please the pastor or even those who are present. It is not to stage a concert or a work of art (although music is essential to liturgy which itself is indeed a form of art). Rather, our goal is to create an occasion for people to share in the redeeming and transforming mystery of Christ, to experience in prayer the God whose life we are called to share, who, if we but listen, speaks to us in the liturgy we celebrate.

TABLE OF CONTENTS

THE THREE DAYS: AN INTRODUCTION

Historical Survey

Origins

To have been a member of the early Church was far from a private venture. Essentially it concerned belonging to a group of people who shared a common belief in the teachings and message of Jesus Christ, the Christ who died, whose body was placed in the tomb, who arose from the dead on the third day, and who returned to his Father with a promise to come again. Furthermore, these early believers also shared a common lifestyle, a pattern of living and acting which both baffled and intrigued their contemporaries. A striking characteristic of this minority religious group was that once a week, Saturday evening till Sunday (on what was called the "first day of the week" or the Lord's Day) its adherents assembled together — listening to the sacred texts (the memoirs of the apostles and the writings of the prophets) and then sharing a common Eucharistic meal together. It was this weekly cycle, based on Sunday, the day of the Lord's triumph over death, which was the community's sign of what it was and what it hoped to be. Certainly not all the converts were present for this weekly assembly. Nonetheless, the ideal was still beautifully expressed years later by the martyrs of Abitina, a town in Africa: "We cannot live without the Sunday gathering."

Yet already in the second century and in Asia Minor we find another feast developing, this time an annual celebration of Christ's victory over death by means of his Resurrection. It is very likely that the early converts from Judaism continued to observe the Passover, a feast which was so important in their Jewish religious lives. Furthermore, these new Christians surely viewed this traditional Jewish observance through the eyes of their new-found faith in the Lord. The gospel accounts tell us that the Passion, death, burial, and Resurrection of Christ occurred at the time of the Jewish Passover. Jesus, we are told, died at the very hour when the paschal lambs were being sacrificed in the temple. The Lord's last meal was in all probability a Passover meal. "Christ our paschal lamb has been sacrificed" (1 Cor 5:7). There can be little doubt that the early Christian converts from Judaism gradually and increasingly came to link their new religious outlook with their Jewish religious heritage and practice. Although explicit documentary evidence is scant, there is convincing testimony pointing to a solemn annual observance, linked to the Passover, on the part of the Christian community.

Date of the Feast

One area giving us indirect evidence as to the existence of this annual feast is a dispute concerning the date of the feast. We know that early in the second century the Jewish Christians living in Asia Minor observed this annual feast on 14 Nisan according to the Jewish calendar. The Jewish Passover always fell on 14 Nisan, and so these Jewish converts celebrated the feast on the 14 Nisan, no matter on what day of the week this occurred. Called *quartodecimans* (from the Latin for 14), their focus was more on the death of Christ, and they claimed that their celebration on this date came from no other authority than that of St. John the Apostle. Other churches (including Rome) focused more on the Resurrection and celebrated on the Sunday after 14 Nisan. Factions were soon to arise (the idea of a highly unified Church in the early centuries is pure romanticism); Pope Victor (c. 189–198) intervened; threats of excommunication ensued; some bishops called for mutual toleration; a synod was called. At any rate, by the third century the question seems to have been settled, especially after the Council of Nicaea (325), which determined that the celebration should take place on the first Sunday after the first full moon after the spring equinox. Nonetheless, the quartodecimans survived down to the fifth century. Whatever else may be said about this dispute, it shows how seriously the early Christians viewed this feast. Differences concerning the calculation of this annual feast (Easter) continued for centuries. For those following the Gregorian calendar, formulated by Pope Gregory XIII in 1582, the celebration may occur between 22 March and 25 April; for those Eastern Christians who follow the more ancient Julian calendar, the feast usually occurs after the western observance.

The Name

From early on, this annual feast of Christ's death and Resurrection was called the Pascha or Pasch (from the Greek *pascha*, which in turn comes from the Hebrew *pesach*). The Hebrew, literally meaning "passage," relates to Exodus 12:11 and Numbers 28:16 where YHWH (the LORD) or the LORD's angels pass over the homes of the Israelites in Egypt. The term Pasch was used for both the ancient Jewish as well as the new Christian observances.

The Meaning

A close examination of the few early documents that have come down to us shows that different areas focused their theology or understanding of the feast in different ways. Jewish tradition understood the Passover in two ways: that of God "passing over" and that of the Jewish people passing from slavery to freedom. In

Christian tradition it becomes the "passover" or Passion of Jesus Christ and the Christian passing over from death to life. Although a unity of the mystery of salvation is always seen, the spiritual filter often changes from church to church. As already noted, for Asia Minor it was the death and suffering. For St. Irenaeus (c. 130–c. 200) in Gaul, an area which observed the feast on Sunday, Christ's Resurrection seems to have been highlighted. In some areas emphasis was on Christ's passage; elsewhere it was our passage with Christ; in other places it is Christ's descent into hell and his struggle with the powers of darkness. Often there is a pronounced eschatological thrust: Christ's Resurrection is the pledge of our future resurrection.

Shape of the Vigil

Due to the dearth of sources, we have little knowledge as to the details of the shape or structure of the celebration. We do know, however, that it was a night watch, a full vigil extending to sunrise the following morning. The first part of the service consisted of readings, psalms, preaching, and prayers. This was followed by the Eucharist, still part of a meal or separate from it. In time Baptism came to be celebrated during this night, the newly baptized being, as one author puts it, "breathing icons of the risen Christ." The first explicit testimony of baptisms celebrated during the Vigil seems to have been given by Tertullian (c. 160–c. 220) in Africa, with the practice of baptizing at Easter, and in some areas also at Pentecost, becoming common in the fourth century.

Fasting

One of the most expressive elements of the early Pascha was that the faithful fasted one or two days (in some areas even up to a week) before the celebration. This fast, called the "core" of every Christian fast, was serious business indeed. It was very, very strict and uninterrupted. If unable to be kept at the regular time, the discipline was, at least in some places, observed after Pentecost. It was only with the Vigil that the fast was broken. The meaning of this ascetical practice, at least according to Tertullian (c. 160–c. 220) was that a person fasts because the bridegroom has been taken away. The Christian goes from fast to feast. The fast is eschatological, broken by participation in the Eucharist which is a foretaste of the heavenly banquet.

Pentecost

From at least the early years of the third century the feast of the Lord's Resurrection extended onward for fifty days (Pentecost). This period of time, the oldest liturgical season of the Church year, was, as it were, a continuous feast, an extension of Easter joy, a Sunday extending for fifty days, a prolongation of what had been celebrated. It was a time when customary penitential practices like kneeling and fasting were put aside. These days, constituting a week of weeks, were seen as prefiguring eternity. The fast is over; now is the time to rejoice since the Savior has risen. By the end of the third century more and more emphasis was placed on the concluding days of the observance, and from the middle of the fourth century there began to appear special commemorations of the Ascension and Pentecost Sunday itself.

Jerusalem

After Constantine the Great (274 or 288–337) granted freedom to Christianity (contrary to what is sometimes stated, he did not make Christianity the official state religion), the Church no longer existed as a persecuted and marginal group. The Emperor, although baptized only shortly before his death, was a pious, believing man who constructed buildings for worship. Consequently people could express their faith in public, not only in Rome and Constantinople but also in Jerusalem where most of the inhabitants were now Christians; the Emperor Hadrian (117–138) had forbidden Jews not only from living in the city but also even from visiting it. At certain times of the year Jerusalem's Christian population swelled as pilgrims from Europe came to visit the holy sites. One such visitor, a Spanish nun named Egeria, left us a narrative, unfortunately incomplete, of her visit to Jerusalem and elsewhere in the east. Probably written between 394 and 417, the document describes the Jerusalem liturgy and especially the liturgies of Holy Week when the faithful gathered on Palm Sunday, Holy Thursday, Good Friday, Easter night, etc. What we find here is a type of "travelling" liturgy as the people moved from place to place, from shrine to shrine or church to church connected with the actual events of the Lord's Passion and Resurrection. What some see here is a historicizing tendency, a celebration of each step taken by Christ on the way to the Resurrection. Several times a day (for example on Holy Thursday and Good Friday) the people gathered for prayer or for liturgical celebration. As pilgrims like Egeria returned home to the west, they brought with them the memories of what they had seen in Jerusalem. And so a liturgical migration took place. What was done in Jerusalem influenced western local practice. The primitive paschal celebration continued to be celebrated, but people also began to hold, following Jerusalem practice, liturgies on the Thursday and Friday before the Vigil.

We should remember that liturgical practice often differed from one local church to another. Strict liturgical conformity was not an object of concern. Certainly there were general ritual patterns: for example, all Christians shared the table of God's word and participated at the table of the Eucharist; Baptism included a water rite together with some type of baptismal formula; a bishop was ordained by the laying on of hands and an invocatory prayer. Yet at an early period, regional patterns of liturgy developed, often centered around an important city (for example, Milan, Toledo, Alexandria, Jerusalem). There was no liturgical office in Rome overseeing liturgical developments. The bishop was trusted to know what was appropriate for his diocese. And so it was that much diversity and local freedom existed as local churches in the west began to observe Holy Thursday and Good Friday before the all-important Saturday night Vigil. The history of the celebrations prior to the Vigil and even the rites of the Vigil itself form a mosaic of local traditions and general practice.

The Triduum

The most ancient designation for the days on which the Church observed, either by ritual, by fasting, or by both, the death and resurrection of Christ is *triduum* (*tres dies*, i.e., three days). St. Ambrose (c. 339–397) speaks of a "sacred triduum" on which Christ "suffered and rested and rose." In Africa St. Augustine (354–430) speaks of the "most holy triduum of the crucified, buried, and risen Lord." The days designated by Triduum were Friday, Saturday, and Sunday. But once the ceremonies of the Vigil were, during the Middle Ages, shifted to Holy Saturday morning, Holy Thursday became part of the Triduum in order to fill out the span of three days: Thursday, Friday, Saturday. It was only in the 1930s that the expressions "Easter Triduum" and "Paschal Triduum" came into use. Today the Triduum begins on Holy Thursday evening and concludes with evening prayer on Easter Sunday.

Middle Ages

During the Middle Ages the Triduum underwent a period of disintegration whose aftermath would continue down to the middle of the twentieth century. The services came to be celebrated early in the morning, with only a few pious people attending. Priest, servers, and a few of the laity gathered at a time of day that *anticipated* events in Christ's life, for example, the commemoration of the crucifixion early on Friday morning. Furthermore, the powerful symbolism (e.g., that of light and darkness) was simply lost when celebrating what was to be a night vigil at 7:30 in the morning.

Such anomalies were carried over into the 1570 Missal of Pope Pius V, which was issued after the Council of Trent. This was the book to be followed by all the churches of the Roman Rite except for those possessing a local liturgy that was over two hundred years old.

Modern Reforms

Historical investigation into the origins and development of Christian worship began well before the nineteenth century. Study of the sermons, dogmatic tracts, and other writings of the Church Fathers, research upon various early Church documents and early medieval liturgical books — all contributed to an increasing understanding of the Church's liturgical traditions in both East and West. Especially in the twentieth century there developed an interest in the pastoral aspects of liturgy, with a focus on liturgical instruction and participation by the people. These two currents, one historical and the other pastoral, resulted in what has been called the "liturgical movement." Contributing to this movement was an increasing interest in patristics, Scripture, and catechetics.

One of the earliest fruits of the liturgical movement was the 1951 reform, "by way of experiment" and at the discretion of the bishop, of the Easter Vigil, which was henceforth to be held in the evening. Then on 16 November 1955 a reform of all Holy Week was issued by Rome, a reform anticipating some of the postconciliar reforms that, as it were, came to be codified in the 1970 Roman Missal, the book containing the rites observed today for the Triduum. One constant feature of all these reforms is the primacy of the assembly, from the times appointed for the celebration of the various liturgies to emphasis on the active participation of the people.

Documentation

Circular Letter "Paschalis sollemnitatis"

1   The Easter Solemnity, revised and restored by Pius XII in 1951, and then the Order of Holy Week in 1955, were favorably received by the Church of the Roman Rite.

The Second Vatican Council, especially in the Constitution on the Sacred Liturgy, repeatedly drawing upon tradition called attention to Christ's Paschal Mystery and pointed out that it is the font from which all sacraments and sacramentals draw their power.

2   Just as the week has its beginning and climax in the celebration of Sunday, which always has a paschal character, so the summit of the whole liturgical year is in the sacred Easter Triduum of the Passion and Resurrection of the Lord, which is prepared for by the period of Lent and prolonged for fifty days.

3   In many parts of the Christian world, the faithful followers of Christ, with their pastors, attach great importance to the celebration of this rite, and participate in it with great spiritual gain.

However, in some areas where initially the reform of the Easter Vigil was received enthusiastically, it would appear that with the passage of time this enthusiasm has begun to wane. The very concept of the vigil has almost come to be forgotten in some places with the result that it is celebrated as if it were an evening Mass, in the same way and at the same time as the Mass celebrated on Saturday evening in anticipation of the Sunday.

It also happens that the celebrations of the Triduum are not held at the correct times. This is because certain devotions and pious exercises are held at more convenient times and so the faithful participate in them rather than in the liturgical celebrations.

Without any doubt one of the principal reasons for this state of affairs is the inadequate formation given to the clergy and the faithful regarding the Paschal Mystery as the center of the liturgical year and of Christian life.

4   The holiday period which today in many places coincides with Holy Week, and certain attitudes held by present-day society, concur to present difficulties for the faithful to participate in these celebrations.

27   During Holy Week the Church celebrates the mysteries of salvation accomplished by Christ in the last days of his life on earth, beginning with his messianic entrance into Jerusalem.

The Lenten season lasts until the Thursday of this week. The Easter Triduum begins with the evening Mass of the Lord's Supper, is continued through Good Friday with the celebration of the Passion of the Lord and Holy Saturday, reaches its summit in the Easter Vigil, and concludes with Vespers of Easter Sunday.

"The days of Holy Week, from Monday to Thursday inclusive, have precedence over all other celebrations." It is not fitting that Baptisms and Confirmations be celebrated on these days.

38   The greatest mysteries of the redemption are celebrated yearly by the Church beginning with the evening Mass of the Lord's Supper on Holy Thursday until Vespers of Easter Sunday. This time is called "the triduum of the crucified, buried and risen"; it is also called the "Easter Triduum" because during it is celebrated the Paschal Mystery, that is,

the passing of the Lord from this world to his Father. The Church by the celebration of this mystery, through liturgical signs and sacramentals, is united to Christ her Spouse in intimate communion.

41 For the celebration of the Easter Triduum it is necessary that there be a sufficient number of ministers and assistant who are prepared so that they know what their role is in the celebration. Pastors must ensure that the meaning of each part of the celebration be explained to the faithful so that they may participate more fully and fruitfully.

42 The chants of the people and also of the ministers and the celebrating priest are of special importance in the celebration of Holy Week and particularly of the Easter Triduum because they add to the solemnity of these days, and also because the texts are more effective when sung.

The Episcopal Conferences are asked, unless provision has already been made, to provide music for those parts which should always be sung, namely:

a) The General Intercessions of Good Friday, the deacon's invitation and the acclamation of the people;

b) chants for the showing and veneration of the cross;

c) the acclamations during the procession with the paschal candle and the Easter proclamation, the responsorial "Alleluia the litany of the saints, and the acclamation after the blessing of water.

Since the purpose of sung texts is also to facilitate the participation of the faithful, they should not be lightly omitted; such texts should be set to music. If the text for use in the liturgy has not yet been set to music it is possible as a temporary measure to select other similar texts which are set to music. It is, however, fitting that there should be a collection of texts set to music for these celebrations, paying special attention to:

a) chants for the procession and blessing of palms, and for the entrance into church;

b) chants to accompany the procession with the Holy Oils;

c) chants to accompany the procession with the gifts on Holy Thursday in the evening Mass of the Lord's Supper, and hymns to accompany the profession of the Blessed Sacrament to the place of repose;

d) the responsorial psalms at the Easter Vigil, and chants to accompany the sprinkling with blessed water.

Music should be provided for the passion narrative, the Easter proclamation, and the blessing of baptismal water; obviously the melodies should be of a simple nature in order to facilitate their use.

In larger churches where the resources permit, a more ample use should be made of the Church's musical heritage both ancient and modern, always ensuring that this does not impede the active participation of the faithful.

43 It is fitting that small religious communities both clerical and lay, and other lay groups should participate in the celebration of the Easter Triduum in neighboring principal churches.

Similarly where the number of participants and ministers is so small that the celebrations of the Easter Triduum cannot be carried out with the requisite solemnity, such groups of the faithful should assemble in a larger church.

Also where there are small parishes with only one priest, it is recommended that such parishes should assemble, as far as possible, in a principal church and there participate in the celebrations.

According to the needs of the faithful, where a pastor has the responsibility for two or more parishes in which the faithful assemble in large numbers, and where the celebrations can be carried out with the requisite care and solemnity, the celebrations of the Easter Triduum may be repeated in accord with the given norms.

So that seminary students "might live fully Christ's Paschal Mystery, and thus be able to teach those who will be committed to their care," they should be given a thorough and comprehensive liturgical formation. It is important that during their formative years in the seminary they should experience fruitfully the solemn Easter celebrations, especially those over which the bishop presides.

Universal Norms on the Liturgical Year and the Calendar

1 Holy Church celebrates the saving work of Christ on prescribed days in the course of the year with sacred remembrance. Each week, on the day

called the Lord's Day, she commemorates the Resurrection of the Lord, which she also celebrates once a year in the great Paschal Solemnity, together with his blessed Passion. In fact, throughout the course of the year the Church unfolds the entire mystery of Christ and observes the birthdays of the Saints.

During the different periods of the liturgical year, in accord with traditional discipline, the Church completes the education of the faithful by means of both spiritual and bodily devotional practices, instruction, prayer, works of penance, and works of mercy.

18   Since Christ accomplished his work of human redemption and of the perfect glorification of God principally through his Paschal Mystery, in which by dying he has destroyed our death, and by rising restored our life, the sacred Paschal Triduum of the Passion and Resurrection of the Lord shines forth as the high point of the entire liturgical year. Therefore the preeminence that Sunday has in the week, the Solemnity of Easter has in the liturgical year.

Instruction "Musicam sacram" on music in the liturgy

66   Solo playing of musical instruments is forbidden during . . . the Easter triduum . . .

Roman Missal

1   In the Sacred Triduum, the Church solemnly celebrates the greatest mysteries of our redemption, keeping by means of special celebrations the memorial of her Lord, crucified, buried, and risen.

The Paschal Fast should also be kept sacred. It is to be celebrated everywhere on the Friday of the Lord's Passion and, where appropriate, prolonged also through Holy Saturday as a way of coming, with spirit uplifted, to the joys of the Lord's Resurrection.

2   For a fitting celebration of the Sacred Triduum, a sufficient number of lay ministers is required, who must be carefully instructed as to what they are to do.

The singing of the people, the ministers, and the Priest Celebrant has a special importance in the celebrations of these days, for when texts are sung, they have their proper impact.

Pastors should, therefore, not fail to explain to the Christian faithful, as best they can, the meaning and order of the celebrations and to prepare them for active and fruitful participation.

3   The celebrations of the Sacred Triduum are to be carried out in cathedral and parochial churches and only in those churches in which they can be performed with dignity, that is, with a good attendance of the faithful, an appropriate number of ministers, and the means to sing at least some of the parts.

Consequently, it is desirable that small communities, associations, and special groups of various kinds join together in these churches to carry out the sacred celebrations in a more noble manner.

Reflection

The Paschal Triduum, called the very heart of the liturgical year, contains the most solemn celebrations of the Church year. Just as Sunday gives meaning to the week that follows, so the Triduum is the focal point and very center of the Church's yearly cycle of feasts and seasons.

God's plan for the world was revealed in Jesus Christ who took on human form so that he might "dwell among us" (Jn 1:14). While this human existence of the Word extended from the Lord's initial appearance on earth to his glorious Ascension into heaven, the very core of Christ's mission is to be found in his death and resurrection. By dying and rising God's Son broke the bonds of death and was restored to life. He passed through pain and darkness so that he might lead us to the fullness of light.

Nonetheless, what Christ accomplished, his total self-giving, does not remain isolated in the past, shut up, as it were, in the confines of history. Nor is the Triduum liturgy merely a commemoration of a past event, for the power of Christ's actions remains; it continues on. So it is that through the liturgy we participate in Christ's victory over sin and death. What Christ did some nineteen centuries ago has a presence, a power, an ongoing effect. It happens in us today, and it also looks forward to the future, to the time of Christ's second coming, to the time of our own bodily resurrection. During these holy days we celebrate not only Christ's passover but also — joined as we are to him — our own passover, for what we celebrate are not the historical moments of Christ's life but his saving mystery in which we participate.

The climax of the Triduum is the Paschal Vigil during which the community welcomes and initiates new members through Baptism, Confirmation, and the Eucharist. It was not by accident that initiation came to be associated with this celebration since it is by reason of Baptism that we share in the power of Christ's triumphant resurrection. As St. Paul so wonderfully expressed it, "Do you not know that all of us who have been baptized into Christ were baptized into his death? Therefore we have been buried with him by baptism into death, so that, just as Christ was raised from the dead by the glory of the Father, so we too might walk in newness of life" (Rom 6:3–4).

Suggested Questions for Discussion

1   When should planning for the Easter Triduum begin?

2   Why is it important to plan for the overall season of Lent? Triduum? Fifty Days?

3   How can the celebration of the Triduum be made to appear as a unitive celebration?

4   What principle or principles would govern the choice of which parts of the liturgy are to be sung?

5   May the Triduum celebrations be repeated on the same day in a parish?

6   What special challenges exist regarding the Triduum in parishes customarily having separate liturgies for various language groups?

7   Why is it especially important that the ministers during the Triduum represent all ethnic groups in the parish? What qualifications should these ministers have?

8   Is the role of the deacon especially important during the Triduum?

9   In places where there is no priest, may the deacon preside at any of the Triduum celebrations? If so, what does this say about the Triduum as a whole?

10   What part should the catechumens play in the Thursday and Friday celebrations of the Triduum?

11   It has been said that the best catechesis of the Triduum is its exquisite celebration. What does this mean in regard to the symbols used during these days?

12   Many processions occur during the Triduum. What elements contribute to an orderly and well-planned procession?

Bibliography

- *Days of the Lord: The Liturgical Year*, vol. 3, *Easter Triduum, Easter Season*. Collegeville: The Liturgical Press, 1993.
- "Eighteen Questions on the Paschal Triduum." *CDW Newsletter* 46 (February 2010).
- "Fourteen Questions on the Paschal Triduum." *BCL Newsletter* 41 (February 2005).
- Jews and Judaism in the Liturgies of Lent and Holy Week." *BCL Newsletter* 42 (February 2006).
- "Lent and Holy Week Helps." *National Bulletin on Liturgy* 6:37. Complete issue.
- "Preparing for the Easter Triduum." *BCL Newsletter* 32 (January 1998).
- "Proposed Adaptations for the Rites of Holy Week and the Easter Triduum." *BCL Newsletter* 32 (April 1996).
- "The Celebration of Penance on Good Friday and Holy Saturday." *BCL Newsletter* 14 (January 1978).
- "The Celebration of the Sacraments during the Easter Triduum." *BCL Newsletter* 14 (January 1978).
- "The Paschal Triduum." *Liturgy* 11 (Spring 1994) 29–46.
- "The Three Days of Easter." *Assembly* 6 (March 1980) 81.
- "The Three Days of Pascha." *Assembly* 18 (January 1992). Complete issue.
- Adam, Adolf. *The Key to Faith: Meditations on the Liturgical Year*, tr. Patrick Madigan. Collegeville: The Liturgical Press, 1998.
- Baldovin, John F. "Holy Week, Liturgies of." In *The New Dictionary of*
- *Sacramental Worship*, ed. Peter E. Fink. Collegeville: The Liturgical Press, 1990. 542–552.
- Buxton, R.F. "Holy Week." In *The New Westminster Dictionary of Liturgy and Worship*, ed. J.G. Davies. Philadelphia: The Westminster Press, 1986. 259–260.
- Cantalamessa, Raniero. *The Mystery of Easter*, tr. Alan Neame. Collegeville: The Liturgical Press, 1993.
- Chittister, Joan D. "Whose Drama Is It, Anyway?" *Pastoral Music* 13 (August–September 1989) 19–21.
- Cobb, Peter G. "The History of the Christian Year." In *The Study of Liturgy*, revised edition, ed. Cheslyn Jones and others. New York: Oxford University Press, 1992. 455–472.
- Crichton, J.D. *The Liturgy of Holy Week*, revised edition. Dublin: Veritas Publications, 1983.
- DePaoli, Edward M. "Symbols Clash in Holy Week." *Living Worship* 16 (March 1980).

- Field, James. "The Paschal Fast: Good Friday & Beyond." *Assembly* 6 (March 1980).
- Halmo, Joan. "Hymns for the Paschal Triduum." *Worship* 55 (March 1981) 137–159.
- Halmo, Joan. "Planning Lent, Triduum, Eastertime: A Survey of Pastoral Guidebooks." *Worship* 56 (January 1982) 16–27.
- Huck, Gabe. *The Three Days: Parish Prayer in the Paschal Triduum*. Chicago: Liturgy Training Publications, 1992.
- Huck, Gabe and Mary Ann Simcoe, eds. *A Triduum Sourcebook*. Chicago: Liturgy Training Publications, 1983.
- Huels, John M. "Be Sure to Read the Footnotes." *Pastoral Music* 14:3 (February-March 1990) 67–68.
- Huels, John M. "Preparing and Celebrating the Paschal Feasts." *Worship* 63:1 (January 1989) 71–78.
- Jounel, P. "The Easter Cycle." In *The Church at Prayer: An Introduction to the Liturgy*. New Edition, ed. A.G. Martimort, vol. 4. Collegeville: The Liturgical Press, 1986. 33–76.
- Keyl, Timothy J. "The Music of the Season." *Liturgy* 11 (Fall 1993) 99–103.
- Marchal, Michael H. "The Rites of the Season". *Liturgy* 11 (Fall 1993) 71–83.
- Neumann, Don. *Holy Week in the Parish*. (American Essays on Liturgy) Collegeville: The Liturgical Press, 1991.
- Nocent, Adrian. *The Liturgical Year*, vol. 3, tr. Matthew J. O'Connell. Collegeville, MN: The Liturgical Press, 1977.
- Notebaart, James. "We Need to Understand that 'the Triduum Is a Single Celebration of the Paschal Mystery'," *Pastoral Music* 19 (April-May 1995) 19–27.
- Pastoral Music Staff. "Here's How We Sing the Paschal Mystery." *Pastoral Music* 19 (April-May 1995) 47–50.
- Power, David N. "Crucified, Buried, and Risen." *Pastoral Music* 14 (February-March 1990) 23–26.
- Regan, Patrick. "The Three Days and the Forty Days." Worship 54 (January 1980) 2–18.
- Sloyan, Gerard. "The Paschal Triduum: An Enduring Drama." *Pastoral Music* 13 (August-September 1989) 15–18.
- Stevenson, Kenneth. *Jerusalem Revisited: The Liturgy of Holy Week*. Washington DC: The Pastoral Press, 1988.
- Strusinski, Robert. "Music for the Three Days." *Pastoral Music* 13 (August-September 1989) 31–33.
- Talley, Thomas J. "History and Eschatology in the Primitive Pascha." In *Worship: Reforming Tradition*. Washington, DC: The Pastoral Press, 1990. 75–86.
- Talley, Thomas J. *The Origins of the Liturgical Year*. New York: Pueblo Publishing Company, 1986.

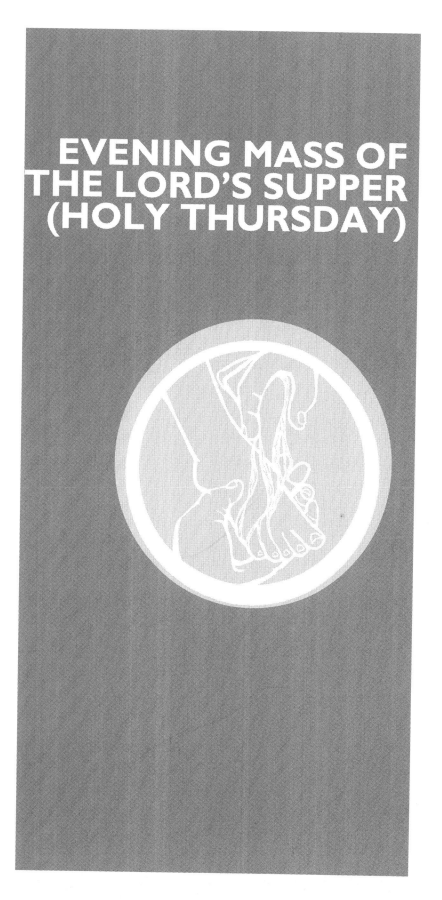

EVENING MASS OF THE LORD'S SUPPER (HOLY THURSDAY)

Evening Mass of the Lord's Supper (Holy Thursday)

Opening Rites

LITURGY OF THE WORD
First Reading
Psalm Response
Second Reading
Gospel Acclamation
Gospel
Homily
Washing of Feet
General Intercessions

LITURGY OF THE EUCHARIST
Preparation Rite
Eucharistic Prayer
Communion Rite

The Transfer of the Most Blessed Sacrament

Introduction

Historical Survey

Few feasts in the liturgical calendar have experienced such a varied and complex history as Holy Thursday, whose evening Mass of the Lord's Supper is the solemn opening of the Easter Triduum. Even the various names given to this day throughout history attest to its various motifs. Today's official designation is *feria quinta in coena Domini* (Thursday of the Last Supper). In England this day is known as "Maundy Thursday," from the command (*mandatum*) that we love one another; in Germany it is called *Gründonnerstag* (Weeping Thursday) from *greinden* (to cry), a designation perhaps connected with the ancient custom of reconciling penitents on this day. In the fifth-century calendar of Polemius Silvius it is called the *natalis calicis* ("birth of the chalice"); elsewhere its name was *natale sacramenti* ("birth of the sacrament"). Some areas referred to it as "Thursday of the Old Passover." Finally, the day was also known as the *dies traditionis* (either the day of the betrayal by Judas, or the day when Jesus handed over himself in death or handed himself over in the Eucharist, or the day when Christians hand themselves over to the Lord).

Historically, Holy Thursday stood at numerous liturgical crossroads: it became the last Eucharistic day before the Easter Vigil; it was the last day of the original forty day period of Lent; it was the day of the Eucharistic institution; it was the day on which sinners received absolution; it was the day on which the Lord's Passion began. All these currents would eventually interact with and contribute to the many liturgical structures that came to be celebrated on Holy Thursday.

Initially, the only special practice observed by Christians on this Thursday was fasting, this being part of the strict fast before the Vigil itself. Yet by the end of the fourth century the Eucharist came to be celebrated on this day. In Jerusalem the bishop and people gathered during the afternoon in the Basilica of the Martyrium where Mass was celebrated to conclude the Lenten fast; the assembly then proceeded to Calvary where the faithful recalled the institution of the Eucharist. The Council of Carthage (397) in Africa speaks of the Eucharist being celebrated on this day, and St. Augustine (354–430) says that some celebrate Mass on Thursday morning to break their Lenten fast whereas there is still another celebration in the evening after supper.

As to Rome, we know that in the fourth century those doing public penance were reconciled on this day, thus lightening the ceremonies of the Easter Vigil itself, and yet this reconciliation seemingly did not take place within a Mass. But by the seventh century an extensive evolution seems to have taken place. In the morning the people went to their local churches where a Mass ending the Lenten fast was celebrated. Then at midday those who were able gathered at the Lateran Basilica, the church where the pope then resided and which still remains the cathedral church of Rome. It was here that the pontiff celebrated a Mass during which he blessed the oils in preparation for the Easter Vigil; this Mass originally lacked a liturgy of the word. Then in the evening the people returned to their own parishes for a Mass commemorating the institution of the Eucharist at the Last Supper.

Through a series of liturgical adjustments only one Mass came to be celebrated; it commemorated the Last Supper and during it the bishop in his cathedral blessed the oils to be used during the Vigil and throughout the year.

Down through the centuries the time for the celebration of the Holy Thursday Mass varied from place to place. Yet once Pope Pius V (pope from 1566–1572) decreed that Mass could not be celebrated in the afternoon, the Holy Thursday celebration was restricted to the morning hours. The 1955 revision of Holy Week specified that a special Mass for consecrating the chrism and holy oils take place in the morning in the cathedral, whereas the Mass recalling the institution of the Eucharist occurs "in the evening, at a convenient hour."

The 1970 reform of the liturgy greatly altered the atmosphere of the celebration. Although a type of concelebration — for example, at Orleans in France toward the end of the Middle Ages six canons (diocesan clergy attached to a cathedral) joined the bishop in singing the presider's text (except for the words of institution) — it was not till 1970 that priests were to concelebrate on this day and not remain part of the faithful at large as formerly. Additionally, the restoration of communion under both kinds, already allowed in special circumstances since 1965, focused special attention upon Christ's command to "take and eat . . . take and drink." Communion from the cup, however, did not become a general practice in the United States until 1978.

The relationship of Holy Thursday to the structure of the Triduum has shifted down through history. Originally the day before the Triduum during which one recalled the "death, burial, and resurrection of Christ" (Friday, Saturday, Sunday), Thursday came to be seen as part of the Triduum itself (Thursday, Friday, Saturday) once the vigil ceremonies were celebrated early Saturday morning. Today the Holy Thursday evening celebration, the Mass of the Lord's Supper, begins the Triduum which itself extends to Easter Sunday afternoon when Evening Prayer is celebrated.

Documentation

Circular Letter "Paschalis sollemnitatis"

44 With the celebration of Mass on the evening of Holy Thursday "the Church begins the Easter Triduum, and recalls the Last Supper, in which the Lord Jesus, on the night he was betrayed, showing his love for those who were his own in the world, he gave his body and blood under the species of bread and wine offering to his Father and giving them to the Apostles so that they might partake of them, and he commanded them and their successors in the priesthood to perpetuate this offering."

46 The Mass of the Lord's Supper is celebrated in the evening, at a time that is more convenient for the full participation of the whole local community. All priests may concelebrate even if on this day they have already concelebrated the Chrism Mass, or if, for the good of the faithful, they must celebrate another Mass.

47 Where pastoral considerations require it, the local Ordinary may permit another Mass to be celebrated in churches and oratories in the evening, and in the case of true necessity, even in the morning, but only for those faithful who cannot otherwise participate in the evening Mass. Care should nevertheless be taken to ensure that celebrations of this kind do not take place for the benefit of private persons or of small groups, and that they are not to the detriment of the main Mass.

According to the ancient tradition of the Church, all Masses without the participation of the people are forbidden on this day.

48 The Tabernacle should be completely empty before the celebration. Hosts for the Communion of the faithful should be consecrated during that celebration. A sufficient amount of bread should be consecrated to provide also for Communion on the following day.

Roman Missal

Thursday of the Lord's Supper
At the Evening Mass

1 The Mass of the Lord's Supper is celebrated in the evening, at a convenient time, with the full participation of the whole local community and with all the Priests and ministers exercising their office.

2   All Priests may concelebrate even if they have already concelebrated the Chrism Mass on this day, or if they have to celebrate another Mass for the good of the Christian faithful.

3   Where a pastoral reason requires it, the local Ordinary may permit another Mass to be celebrated in churches and oratories in the evening and, in case of genuine necessity, even in the morning, but only for the faithful who are in no way able to participate in the evening Mass. Care should, nevertheless, be taken that celebrations of this sort do not take place for the advantage of private persons or special small groups, and do not prejudice the evening Mass.

4   Holy Communion may only be distributed to the faithful during Mass; but it may be brought to the sick at any hour of the day.

5   The altar may be decorated with flowers with a moderation that accords with the character of this day. The tabernacle should be entirely empty; but a sufficient amount of bread should be consecrated in this Mass for the Communion of the clergy and the people on this and the following day.

Reflection

The evening Mass of the Lord's Supper is the solemn and joyful opening of the Easter Triduum. Although today's celebration links us with the past, no attempt is made to recreate the Last Supper. Within the context of the Triduum as a whole, the liturgy — like the three days in general — reflects a unity, that of one Church sharing in the Eucharist and obeying Christ's command to serve one another.

Holy Thursday's focus on the institution of the Eucharist has led some to call this day the "feast of priests." Be this as it may, we do well to recall what an early fourth-century scribe living in either Egypt or Syria wrote in a document called the *Apostolic Church Order*. A paraphrase of the original text is: "The bishop should not exalt himself over the deacons or priests. Nor should the priest exalt himself over the people, for the make-up of the Church depends on one another. For if there were no laity, for whom would the bishop be bishop or the priest be priest?"

Suggested Questions for Discussion

1   What principles determine the time of day for the Holy Thursday celebration in your parish?

2   What atmosphere do you want people to experience upon entering the worship space for this celebration? How might such an atmosphere be brought about?

3   Some parishes use Holy Thursday as a day to reconcile penitents, alienated Catholics, etc., thereby restoring the ancient sequence of sorrow, confession, penance, and reconciliation. Good idea or not?

Bibliography

- "Catholics and the Seder Meal." *BCL Newsletter* 43 (February/March 2007).

- "Holy Thursday and Good Friday and the Missale Romanum." *BCL Newsletter* 39 (March/April 2003).

- "The Washing of Feet on Holy Thursday." *BCL Newsletter* 32 (February 1987).

- "Washing the Feet of the Poor." *National Bulletin on Liturgy* 28:140 (Spring 1995) 61–62.

- Boberek, Aurelius. "Breaking Bread, Washing Feet: The Mandata of Holy Thursday." *Assembly* 18:1 (January 1992) 546–547.

- Burke-Sullivan, Eileen. "Naming the Abuse." *Pastoral Music* 14 (February-March 1990) 27–30.

- Buxton, R.F. "Maundy Thursday." In *The New Westminster Dictionary of Liturgy and Worship*, ed. J.G. Davies. Philadelphia: The Westminster Press, 1986. 366–367.

- Connell, Martin F. "Nisi Pedes, Except for the Feet: Footwashing in the Community of John's Gospel." *Worship* 70:6 (November 1996) 517–531.

- Jeffery, Peter. A New Commandment: Toward a Renewed Rite for the Washing of Feet. Collegeville: The Liturgical Press, 1992.

- Jeffery, Peter. "Mandatum Novum Do Vobis: Towards a Renewal of the Holy Thursday Footwashing Rite." *Worship* 64:2 (March 1990) 107–141.

- Kennedy, Dennis. "The Sacrament of Footwashing: I Have Set You an Example." *Living Worship* 16:3 (April 1980).

- Levine, Etan. "On the Symbolism of the Pedilavium." *American Benedictine Review* 33:1 (March 1982) 21–29.

- Searle, Mark. "Holy Thursday: Opening of the Paschal Feast." *Assembly* 6:4 (March 1980) 82ff.

Opening Rites

Historical Survey

The opening rites for the Mass of the Lord's Supper proceed as in every Mass except for the ringing of the bells during the *Gloria*, which is one of the most ancient examples of Christian hymnody. The use of bells (first mounted on the church wall and then held in the hand) at various places in the liturgy began early in the Middle Ages. Often this ringing was seen as a sign of jubilation as, for example, during the *Sanctus*. The silence of the bells during the Triduum also goes back to the Middle Ages where, according to one ninth-century commentator, it was considered a sign of Christ's humility. For many years wooden clappers, called *tabulae*, rather than bells were used during the Holy Thursday liturgy at the "Holy, holy," the elevations, the "Lamb of God," etc.

Today the bells are rung during the singing of the *Gloria* and are not to be used again till this hymn is sung during the Easter Vigil. As some modern writers express it, we now observe a "fast of the ears" which corresponds to a "fast of the eyes" (in areas that cover crosses and images). Musical instruments may, however, support the singing of the people.

Documentation

Circular Letter "Paschalis sollemnitatis"

50   During the singing of the hymn "Gloria in excelsis" in accordance with local custom, the bells may be rung, and should thereafter remain silent until the "Gloria in excelsis" of the Easter Vigil, unless the Conference of Bishops or the local Ordinary, for a suitable reason, has decided otherwise. During this same period the organ and other musical instruments may be used only for the purpose of supporting the singing.

Roman Missal

6   Entrance Antiphon   (cf. Gal 6:14)
     We should glory in the Cross of our Lord Jesus Christ,
     in whom is our salvation, life and resurrection,
     through whom we are saved and delivered.

7   The *Gloria in excelsis* (Glory to God in the highest) is said. While the hymn is being sung, bells are rung, and when it is finished, they remain silent until the *Gloria in excelsis* of the Easter Vigil, unless, if appropriate, the Diocesan Bishop has decided otherwise. Likewise, during this

same period, the organ and other musical instruments may be used only so as to support the singing.

8 **Collect**
O God, who have called us to participate
in this most sacred Supper,
in which your Only Begotten Son,
when about to hand himself over to death,
entrusted to the Church a sacrifice new for all eternity,
the banquet of his love,
grant, we pray,
that we may draw from so great a mystery,
the fullness of charity and of life.
Through our Lord Jesus Christ, your Son,
who lives and reigns with you in the unity of the Holy Spirit,
one God, for ever and ever.

Reflection

The *Missal*'s entrance antiphon gives us a clue as to the atmosphere of this Mass as well as to the meaning of the whole Triduum: "We should glory in the cross . . ." Lent is now over, and we begin the joyful celebration of the Triduum. As we do so, we look forward to and even anticipate the resurrection. The mood this evening is one of joy (e.g., white vestments) even though this joy will only be fully experienced and expressed during the Easter Vigil.

Suggested Questions for Discussion

1 Should the oils the parish receives from the chrism Mass be carried into the church during the entrance procession? If so, where will they be placed during the liturgy? Confer *The Reception of the Holy Oils Blessed at the Chrism Mass*, found in the *Sacramentary Supplement* (published by Catholic Book Publishing Company and the Liturgical Press).

2 Some parishes request that people bring small bells from home to be rung during the *Gloria*? Good idea or bad idea?

Liturgy of the Word – Readings/Homily

Historical Survey

Beginning the cursus of the Triduum's readings is Exodus 12:1–8, 11–14. This pericope, added to the Holy Thursday liturgy with the publication of the Roman Lectionary in 1969, presents us with the Passover meal, a memorial feast which is the context of the institution of the Eucharist.

The responsorial psalm, Psalm 116, was also added in 1969.

The reading from 1 Corinthians 11:23–26, a traditional text on Holy Thursday, is Paul's account of the Eucharistic institution during the Last Supper.

For centuries the antiphon "I give you a new commandment" was one of the chants sung during the washing of the feet. It now becomes the verse before the gospel.

The gospel is John's account of Jesus washing the feet of the disciples. And as at all Masses there is a homily.

Documentation

Lectionary for Mass

39   Holy Thursday A B C
Evening Mass of the Lord's Supper

First Reading
> *The law regarding the Passover meal.*
A reading from the Book of Exodus   12:1–8, 11–14

The LORD said to Moses and Aaron in the land of Egypt,
"This month shall stand at the head of your calendar;
you shall reckon it the first month of the year.
Tell the whole community of Israel:
On the tenth of this month every one of your families
must procure for itself a lamb, one apiece for each household.
If a family is too small for a whole lamb,
it shall join the nearest household in procuring one
and shall share in the lamb
in proportion to the number of persons who partake of it.
The lamb must be a year-old male and without blemish.
You may take it from either the sheep or the goats.
You shall keep it until the fourteenth day of this month,

and then, with the whole assembly of Israel present,
it shall be slaughtered during the evening twilight.
They shall take some of its blood
and apply it to the two doorposts and the lintel
of every house in which they partake of the lamb.
That same night they shall eat its roasted flesh
with unleavened bread and bitter herbs.

"This is how you are to eat it:
with your loins girt, sandals on your feet and your staff in hand,
you shall eat like those who are in flight.
It is the Passover of the LORD.
For on this same night I will go through Egypt,
striking down every firstborn of the land, both man and beast,
and executing judgment on all the gods of Egypt—I, the LORD!
But the blood will mark the houses where you are.
Seeing the blood, I will pass over you;
thus, when I strike the land of Egypt,
no destructive blow will come upon you.

"This day shall be a memorial feast for you,
which all your generations shall celebrate
with pilgrimage to the LORD, as a perpetual institution."

The word of the Lord.

Responsorial Psalm   Ps 116:12–13, 15–16bc, 17–18
R. (cf. 1 Cor 10:16) Our blessing-cup is a communion with the Blood of Christ.

How shall I make a return to the LORD
for all the good he has done for me?
The cup of salvation I will take up,
and I will call upon the name of the LORD.
R. Our blessing-cup is a communion with the Blood of Christ.

Precious in the eyes of the LORD
is the death of his faithful ones.
I am your servant, the son of your handmaid;
you have loosed my bonds.
R. Our blessing-cup is a communion with the Blood of Christ.

To you will I offer sacrifice of thanksgiving,
and I will call upon the name of the LORD.
My vows to the LORD I will pay
in the presence of all his people.
R. Our blessing-cup is a communion with the Blood of Christ

Second Reading

For as often as you eat this bread and drink the cup,
you proclaim the death of the Lord.

A reading from the first Letter of Saint Paul to the Corinthians   11:23–26

Brothers and sisters:
I received from the Lord what I also handed on to you,
that the Lord Jesus, on the night he was handed over,
took bread, and, after he had given thanks,
broke it and said, "This is my body that is for you.
Do this in remembrance of me."
In the same way also the cup, after supper, saying,
"This cup is the new covenant in my blood.
Do this, as often as you drink it, in remembrance of me."
For as often as you eat this bread and drink the cup,
you proclaim the death of the Lord until he comes.

The word of the Lord.

Verse before the Gospel   Jn 13:34
I give you a new commandment, says the Lord:
love one another as I have loved you.

Gospel
Jesus loved them to the end.
A reading from the holy Gospel according to John   13:1–15

Before the feast of Passover, Jesus knew that his hour had come
to pass from this world to the Father.
He loved his own in the world and he loved them to the end.
The devil had already induced Judas,
son of Simon the Iscariot, to hand him over.
So, during supper, fully aware
that the Father had put everything into his power
and that he had come from God and was returning to God,
he rose from supper and took off his outer garments.
He took a towel and tied it around his waist.
Then he poured water into a basin
and began to wash the disciples' feet
and dry them with the towel around his waist.
He came to Simon Peter, who said to him,
"Master, are you going to wash my feet?"
Jesus answered and said to him,
"What I am doing, you do not understand now,
but you will understand later."
Peter said to him, "You will never wash my feet."
Jesus answered him,
"Unless I wash you, you will have no inheritance with me."

Simon Peter said to him,
"Master, then not only my feet, but my hands and head as well."
Jesus said to him,
"Whoever has bathed has no need except to have his feet washed,
for he is clean all over;
so you are clean, but not all."
For he knew who would betray him;
for this reason, he said, "Not all of you are clean."

So when he had washed their feet
and put his garments back on and reclined at table again,
he said to them, "Do you realize what I have done for you?
You call me 'teacher' and 'master,' and rightly so, for indeed I am.
If I, therefore, the master and teacher, have washed your feet,
you ought to wash one another's feet.
I have given you a model to follow,
so that as I have done for you, you should also do."

The Gospel of the Lord.

Circular Letter "Paschalis sollemnitatis"

45   Careful attention should be given to the mysteries which are commemorated in this Mass: the institution of the Eucharist, the institution of the priesthood, and Christ's command of brotherly love; the homily should explain these points.

Roman Missal

9   After the proclamation of the Gospel, the Priest gives a homily in which light is shed on the principal mysteries that are commemorated in this Mass, namely, the institution of the Holy Eucharist and of the priestly Order, and the commandment of the Lord concerning fraternal charity.

Reflection

The readings of Holy Thursday present us with an overview of the major themes that relate to the Eucharist and to Christ's command that we serve one another. The first selection, a favorite of the Church Fathers in their preaching about Baptism, speaks of the Passover lamb, the Old Testament figure of Jesus Christ who gave himself to us in the Eucharist. It is this love which we, in imitation of Christ, are to extend day in and day out; this is the love that sets us free; this is the love that is at the very basis of our unity, our baptismal unity founded in Christ.

1 How many readers should be employed for today's readings?

2 What should be the specific focus of the homily?

Liturgy of the Word – Washing of feet

Historical Survey

From the earliest days of the Church the washing of another person's feet assumed profound religious meaning. For St. Paul (1 Tim 5:10) washing the feet of "the holy ones" was among the tasks to be performed by widows. But it is in the Gospel of John (13:2–20) that we find Jesus washing the feet (the *pedilavium*) of his disciples. Although commentators point out various levels of meaning in this event, Church tradition has emphasized the humility aspect of this action as well as its servant dimension. Jesus was the "suffering servant" portrayed by the prophet Isaiah.

The impact of this footwashing was so great that by the end of the fourth century the gesture had, in certain areas (Milan, parts of Gaul, but not at Rome), been incorporated into the baptismal rites as a sign of hospitality, of welcome, and of cleansing. Yet this ceremony soon fell out of general use as part of the initiation rites.

Already included in the fifth-century Holy Thursday observance in Jerusalem, the rite quickly spread to Spain and the west. Tradition relates that St. Cuthbert (d. 687) in England removed his shoes only on Holy Thursday for the footwashing. And in Spain the 17th Synod of Toledo (694) bemoaned the fact that the ceremony had already passed into disuse and urged its restoration. At any rate, by the Middle Ages the Holy Thursday footwashing had become quite widespread in abbeys, monasteries, and cathedrals.

Two types of footwashing had evolved. One ceremony involved washing the feet of the poor, who often were also given an alms. The other form was to wash the feet of one's fellow monks and clergy, often with those participating also washing each other's feet. Some religious institutions might have held several such footwashings, for example, one early on in the day for the poor and another in the afternoon for the clerics.

Although not held as part of the Mass itself, the ceremony was given a liturgical context: a reading of the Johannine account, the footwashing itself, versicles and responses, a concluding prayer. It could take place in the monastery's chapter room, in the sacristy, in the church itself.

The seventh-century papal liturgy in Rome had the pope wash the feet of the members of his household, whereas in the thirteenth century papal liturgy the feet of twelve subdeacons were washed.

As to the individuals whose feet were washed, it could include a whole religious community or only a symbolic number of participants. In some cathedrals twelve men were selected; elsewhere thirteen men — according to legend Pope Gregory the Great (c. 540–604) was accustomed to wash the feet of twelve poor men, but one day he noticed that he had washed the feet of a thirteenth man, and, of course, the extra person was an angel in human form. Given the mores of the time, it is very unlikely that women were included among those whose feet men were to wash, and yet in certain convents of female religious, women washed the feet of their sisters in religion.

The Missal of 1570 included directions for the *mandatum* (from the Latin for "commandment") which was to be held "at a convenient time" after the Mass. Most frequently only cathedrals and monasteries observed the ceremony. The Missal does not specify whose feet are to be washed, but the *Caeremoniale* (the book of rubrics for the bishop) speaks of thirteen poor men or thirteen members of the clergy.

The 1955 reform of Holy Week was preceded by much discussion as to whether the *mandatum* should be retained (some believed it meaningless in many cultures today) and where, if kept, it should be located — after the liturgy as previously, during the liturgy, and if during it at which place. The final decision retained the rite "depending on pastoral circumstances," and situated it after the homily. The number of persons whose feet were to be washed was not specified and yet, reflecting the practice of the time, they were to be men ("*viri*").

Documentation

Circular Letter "Paschalis sollemnitatis"

51   The washing of the feet of chosen men which, according to tradition, is performed on this day, represents the service and charity of Christ, who

came "not to be served, but to serve. This tradition should be maintained, and its proper significance explained.

Roman Missal

10   After the Homily, where a pastoral reason suggests it, the Washing of the Feet follows.

11   The men who have been chosen are led by the ministers to seats prepared in a suitable place. Then the Priest (removing his chasuble if necessary) goes to each one, and, with the help of the ministers, pours water over each one's feet and then dries them.

12   Meanwhile some of the following antiphons or other appropriate chants are sung.

Antiphon 1   (Cf. Jn 13:4, 5, 15)
After the Lord had risen from supper
he poured water into a basin
and began to wash the feet of his disciples:
he left them this example.

Antiphon 2   (Jn 13:12, 13, 15)
The Lord Jesus, after eating supper with his disciples,
washed their feet and said to them:
Do you know what I, your Lord and Master, have done for you?
I have given you an example, that you should do likewise.

Antiphon 3   (Cf. Jn 13:6, 7,8)
Lord, are you to wash my feet? Jesus said to him in answer:
If I do not wash your feet, you will have no share with me.

V. So he came to Simon Peter and Peter said to him:
—Lord . . .

V. What I am doing, you do not know for now,
but later you will come to know.
—Lord . . .

Antiphon 4   (Jn 13:14)
If I, your Lord and Master, have washed your feet,
how much more should you wash each other's feet?

Antiphon 5   (Jn 13:35)
This is how all will know that you are my disciples:
if you have love for one another.

V. Jesus said to his disciples:
—This is how . . .

Antiphon 6   (Jn 13:34)
I give you a new commandment,
that you love one another
as I have loved you, says the Lord.

Antiphon 7   (1 Cor 13: 13)
Let faith, hope and charity, these three, remain among you,
but the greatest of these is charity.

V. Now faith, hope and charity, these three, remain;
but the greatest of these is charity.
—Let . . .

Reflection

The Holy Thursday footwashing is neither dramatic imitation nor scriptural reenactment. It is a ritual gesture expressive of our commitment to serve one another in love, peace, and humility. Both the Eucharist and the footwashing are, each in its own distinctive way, sacraments of God's love, sacraments of self-giving. "The principal and traditional meaning of the Holy Thursday *mandatum* . . . is the biblical injunction of Christian charity: Christ's disciples are to love one another. . . . All should obey the Lord's new commandment to love one another *with an abundance of love.* . . ." (*BCL Newsletter*, Feb. 1987)

Suggested Questions for Discussion

1   Is the washing of the feet a forced anachronism in today's society?

2   What details regarding the footwashing need to be attended to before the liturgy?

3   What textual thematics would be appropriate for songs used during the washing?

4   Since the footwashing is something to be seen (a visual sign), what does this imply regarding the use of familiar or unfamiliar songs during the ceremony?

5   Is the washing of one another's hands a suitable substitute for the footwashing?

Liturgy of the Word – General Intercessions

Historical Survey

Among the many liturgical proposals of the Second Vatican Council was that the ancient prayer of the faithful be restored (*Sacrosanctum Concilium*, art. 53). As a result, the general intercessions (a more appropriate name) occur at every Mass. The structure of the prayer requires that all take part: presider, deacon (or other minister), and the assembly. The prayer focuses on the needs of all people and not just on the needs of those participating in the liturgy.

Documentation

Ecumenical Directory

22   It is fitting that prayers for unity be offered regularly at special times, such as . . . Holy Thursday, commemorating the institution of the Eucharist, the sacrament of unity, and the prayers of Jesus Christ the Savior in the upper room for the church and its unity . . .

Roman Missal

13   After the Washing of Feet, the Priest washes and dries his hands, puts the chasuble back on, and returns to the chair, and from there he directs the Universal Prayer.

The Creed is not said.

Reflection

In a sense the general intercessions, serving as a climax to the liturgy of the word, allow all present to respond to God's word through prayer for the whole world. Every Eucharistic assembly — and especially the assembly on this night — is called to extend itself to the whole world in a spirit of unity. The needs of people both far and near are the needs of those who would be, as was Christ, servants of others.

Suggested Questions for Discussion

1 Should the general intercessions be sung?

2 How might the general intercessions relate to the footwashing or to the readings?

Liturgy of the Eucharist – Preparation of the Gifts

Historical Survey

From the earliest centuries it was customary for Christians to bring gifts to the community's gathering. These included not only the bread and wine used for the Eucharist but also items to be given to the poor. Often the gifts for the poor were placed in a side room (called a *sacrarium*) built for this purpose. Such items as grapes, flowers, birds, wheat, and eventually money were brought up to the altar and then distributed to the poor after the celebration.

It is especially on this day, when the faithful explicitly recall Christ's command to love one another, that the Church recommends a procession with "gifts for the poor." Meanwhile the *Ubi caritas* ("Where charity . . .") or another appropriate song is sung. The *Ubi caritas*, formerly one of the antiphons that in the twelfth and thirteenth centuries came to be sung during the footwashing, is an abridgment (reduced from nine to three strophes in the 1570 Missal) of an Italian poem dating from the early Middle Ages. With simplicity and grace it combines Pauline expressions with other texts.

Documentation

Circular Letter "Paschalis sollemnitatis"
52 Gifts for the poor, especially those collected during Lent as the fruit of penance, may be presented in the offertory procession, while the people sing "*Ubi caritas est vera.*"

Roman Missal
14 At the beginning of the Liturgy of the Eucharist, there may be a procession of the faithful in which gifts for the poor may be presented with the bread and wine.

Meanwhile the following, or another appropriate chant, is sung.
Ant. Where true Charity is dwelling, God is present there.
By the love of Christ we have been brought together:
let us find in him our gladness and our pleasure;
may we love him and revere him, God the living,
and in love respect each other with sincere hearts.

Ant. Where true charity is dwelling, God is present there.
So when we as one are gathered all together,
let us strive to keep our minds free of division;
may there be an end to malice, strife and quarrels,
and let Christ our God be dwelling here among us.

Ant. Where true charity is dwelling, God is present there.
May your face thus be our vision, bright in glory,
Christ our God, with all the blessed Saints in heaven:
such delight is pure and faultless, joy unbounded,
which endures through countless ages world without end. Amen.

15 **Prayer over the Offerings**
Grant us, O Lord, we pray,
that we may participate worthily in these mysteries,
for whenever the memorial of this sacrifice is celebrated
the work of our redemption is accomplished.
Through Christ our Lord.

Reflection

The early Church Fathers told their listeners to give to the poor what was saved through fasting. Almsgiving, prayer, and fasting were the principal Lenten practices, with prayer being the wings bringing almsgiving and fasting up to God's throne in heaven. And yet there are other works of love that can continually be brought to the Lord both by individuals and the community at large: visiting the sick, the homebound, the elderly, those in prison. Also to be included are the works of charity and justice, the works of reconciliation and healing. All make up what has been called the liturgy outside the liturgy or, better yet, the "living of the liturgy."

Suggested Questions for Discussion

1   What happens to the gifts once they have been presented to the presider?

2   What lesson does the *Missal*'s instruction regarding "gifts for the poor" have regarding other Eucharistic celebrations during the year?

3   What connection is to be made between the gifts and the community's observance of Lent? How is this connection to be put into practice?

Liturgy of the Eucharist – Eucharistic Prayer

Historical Survey

Today's preface relies upon a text found in an eighteenth-century French missal, and yet much of the formula can be traced back to the ninth century.

If Eucharistic Prayer I is used, there is an insert, of ancient origin, recalling the special character of this day. Such inserts, referring to the feast being celebrated, were quite common during the Middle Ages.

In addition, the institution narrative's introduction is slightly expanded to refer to "this day," namely, the day before the Passion, as the day when the Eucharist itself was instituted.

Documentation

Roman Missal

16   **Preface: The Sacrifice and the Sacrament of Christ**
> It is truly right and just, our duty and our salvation,
> always and everywhere to give you thanks,
> Lord, holy Father, almighty and eternal God,
> through Christ our Lord.
>
> For he is the true and eternal Priest,
> who instituted the pattern of an everlasting sacrifice
> and was the first to offer himself as the saving Victim,
> commanding us to make this offering as his memorial.
> As we eat his flesh that was sacrificed for us,
> we are made strong, and,
> as we drink his Blood that was poured out for us,
> we are washed clean.
>
> And so, with Angels and Archangels,
> with Thrones and Dominions,
> and with all the hosts and Powers of heaven,
> we sing the hymn of your glory,
> as without end we acclaim.

Reflection

It is through the Eucharist that we are not only purified of weakness but also receive an increase in faith, hope, and love. As St. Ambrose phrased it: "And so you hear that as often as the sacrifice is offered, the Lord's death, resurrection, and ascension are signified, as well as the remission of sins. . . . Whoever is wounded requires medicine. The wound is that we are under sin; the medicine is the heavenly and venerable sacrament" (*On the Sacraments* V, 25).

Suggested Questions for Discussion

1 What parts of the Eucharistic Prayer would be appropriately sung on this feast?

2 What memorial acclamation would be appropriate?

Liturgy of the Eucharist – Communion Rite

Historical Survey

Historically, the Holy Thursday communion rite is of special interest for two reasons: the absence of the exchange of peace, which has now been restored, and the use of a cup of unconsecrated wine once communion under both kinds ceased to exist.

From the earliest years of Christianity the exchange of peace did not occur on this day. Tertullian (c. 160–c. 220) in Africa reports that the peace was not exchanged on Friday and Saturday of what we call Holy Week. But why was the gesture not given on Thursday, once this day began to have a Eucharistic celebration? Perhaps this was merely an extension, especially once Holy Thursday came to be considered as part of the Triduum. At any rate, medieval commentators attribute this omission to the fact that Judas dishonored the kiss with his treason.

Second, the Vatican II liturgical reforms restored the practice of receiving the consecrated wine from the cup, thus reviving an ancient tradition, one which was faithful to the Lord's command to "take and eat . . . take and drink." But for centuries after communion from the cup disappeared from general practice, in some places the custom survived, as it were, on Holy Thursday when the members of the community received, after communion and from a minister other than the presider, a cup containing unconsecrated wine. At present and especially on Holy Thursday, thanks to Vatican II, all members of the community may share from the cup, a practice that Church tradition has long interpreted as the guarantee and expectation of the heavenly banquet (see Mk 26:29), an understanding so well stated in today's Prayer after Communion.

Documentation

Circular Letter "Paschalis sollemnitatis"

48 The Tabernacle should be completely empty before the celebration. Hosts for the Communion of the faithful should be consecrated during that celebration. A sufficient amount of bread should be consecrated to provide also for Communion on the following day.

53 It is more appropriate that the Eucharist be borne directly from the altar by the deacons, or acolytes, or extraordinary ministers at the moment of communion for the sick and infirm who must communicate at home, so that in this way they may be more closely united to the celebrating Church.

Instruction "Tres abhinc annos"

14 The faithful receiving communion at the chrism Mass on Holy Thursday may receive again at the evening Mass on the same day.

Holy Communion and Worship of the Eucharist Outside Mass

16a On Holy Thursday communion may be given only during Mass; communion may be brought to the sick at any hour of the day.

Roman Missal

33 At an appropriate moment during Communion, the Priest entrusts the Eucharist from the table of the altar to Deacons or acolytes or other extraordinary ministers, so that afterwards it may be brought to the sick who are to receive Holy Communion at home.

34 **Communion Antiphon**   I Cor. 11:24-25
This is the Body that will be given up for you;
this is the Chalice of the new covenant in my Blood, says the Lord;
do this, whenever you receive it, in memory of me.

35   After the distribution of Communion, a ciborium with hosts for Communion on the following day is left on the altar. The Priest, standing at the chair, says the Prayer after Communion.

36   **Prayer after Communion**
Grant, almighty God,
that, just as we are renewed
by the Supper of your Son in this present age,
so we may enjoy his banquet for all eternity.
Who lives and reigns for ever and ever.

Reflection

"The love of Christ that is received as a gift must in turn be given as a gift. Christ's love poured out on us abundantly in the one bread and the one cup must be shared with our neighbor: with the neighbor who is poor and homeless, with the neighbor who is sick or in prison, with the neighbor who belongs to a different . . . race or who does not believe in Christ" (Pope John Paul II, Homily on the occasion of the 43rd International Eucharistic Congress, 18 August 1985).

Suggested Questions for Discussion

1   Does the Eucharistic bread really look like bread?

2   How important is it that communion under both kinds be offered on this day (and other days as well)?

3   Why is it important that communion be distributed with Eucharistic bread consecrated at today's Mass?

4   What is the correct manner of receiving from the cup?

Transfer of the Most Blessed Sacrament

Historical Survey

Since no Mass was celebrated on Good Friday, it was necessary to reserve the consecrated host for the Good Friday communion service. But once the people did not communicate on this day, all that was needed was one large host, which was placed in a cup, covered with a corporal, and simply reserved in the sacristy of the church. The task of taking the Eucharistic bread to this location, being a utilitarian action, was done with the greatest simplicity.

But the rite gradually expanded, especially during the thirteenth to the fifteenth centuries when great emphasis was placed on adoring the Eucharist. The ministers formed a solemn procession; in many places the host was placed in an ornate monstrance and covered with a veil; people said prayers throughout the night before a repository or altar of repose (which was considered to be a type of symbolic tomb for Christ — certainly an anomaly since the Lord was buried on Good Friday after his death on the cross). Additionally, many of the faithful would visit numerous churches where they would a period of adoration before the altar of repose.

Today this rite has been somewhat simplified. There is to be a procession; the Eucharist is reserved in a ciborium or other receptacle, never in a monstrance; the place for reservation is to be simple, not overwhelmed with flowers yet suitably decorated for the occasion; and solemn adoration is not to continue past midnight.

After the procession the altar is stripped. Here we have a vestige of an early practice, perhaps Spanish in origin, of removing the cloth from the altar after each Eucharist. During the Middle Ages it became customary for the priest to recite Psalm 21 (22): "They divide my garments . . ." The altar was seen as the symbol of Christ, and the removal of the altar cloth came to be understood as symbolic of the stripping off of Christ's clothing. Today the ceremony remains, but no text is said.

Along similar lines was the custom, possibly also having its origins in Spain, of washing the altar (and walls, floors, baptismal and holy water fonts, vessels) in preparation for Easter. At times during the Middle Ages wine and water together were used to wash the altar, thus symbolizing the water and blood flowing from the side of Christ. Today this Holy Thursday ceremony occurs only in St. Peter's Basilica in Rome.

Documentation

Circular Letter "Paschalis sollemnitatis"

49 For the reservation of the Blessed Sacrament, a place should be prepared and adorned in such a way as to be conducive to prayer and meditation; seriousness appropriate to the liturgy of these days is enjoined to the avoidance or suppression of all abuses.

When the tabernacle is in a chapel separated from the central part of the church, it is appropriate to prepare the place of repose and adoration there.

54   After the post-communion prayer, the procession forms with the cross-bearer at its head. The Blessed Sacrament, accompanied by lighted candles and incense, is carried through the church to the place of reservation, to the singing of the hymn "*Pange lingua*" or some other Eucharistic song. This rite of transfer of the Blessed Sacrament may not be carried out if the Liturgy of the Lord's passion will not be celebrated in that same church on the following day.

55   The Blessed Sacrament should be reserved in a closed tabernacle or pyx. Under no circumstances may it be exposed in a monstrance.

The place where the tabernacle or pyx is situated must not be made to resemble a tomb, and the expression "tomb" is to be avoided. The chapel of repose is not prepared so as to represent the "Lord's burial" but for the custody of the Eucharistic bread that will be distributed in Communion on Good Friday.

56   After the Mass of the Lord's Supper the faithful should be encouraged to spend a suitable period of time during the night in the church in adoration before the Blessed Sacrament that has been solemnly reserved. Where appropriate, this prolonged Eucharistic adoration may be accompanied by the reading of some part of the Gospel of St. John (chs. 13-17).

From midnight onwards, however, the adoration should be made without external solemnity, for the day of the Lord's passion has begun.

57   After Mass the altar should be stripped. It is fitting that any crosses in the church be covered with a red or purple veil, unless they have already been veiled on the Saturday before the fifth Sunday of Lent. Lamps should not be lit before the images of saints.

Roman Missal

Transfer of the Most Blessed Sacrament

37   After the Prayer after Communion, the Priest puts incense in the thurible while standing, blesses it and then, kneeling, incenses the Blessed Sacrament three times. Then, having put on a white humeral veil, he rises, takes the ciborium, and covers it with the ends of the veil.

38   A procession is formed in which the Blessed Sacrament, accompanied by torches and incense, is carried through the church to a place of repose prepared in a part of the church or in a chapel suitably decorated. A lay minister with a cross, standing between two other ministers with lighted candles leads off. Others carrying lighted candles follow. Before the Priest carrying the Blessed Sacrament comes the thurifer with a smoking thurible. Meanwhile, the hymn *Pange, lingua* (exclusive of the last two stanzas) or another Eucharistic chant is sung.

39   When the procession reaches the place of repose, the Priest, with the help of the Deacon if necessary, places the ciborium in the tabernacle, the door of which remains open. Then he puts incense in the thurible and, kneeling, incenses the Blessed Sacrament, while *Tantum ergo Sacramentum* or another Eucharistic chant is sung. Then the Deacon or the Priest himself places the Sacrament in the tabernacle and closes the door.

40   After a period of adoration in silence, the Priest and ministers genuflect and return to the sacristy.

41   At an appropriate time, the altar is stripped and, if possible, the crosses are removed from the church. It is expedient that any crosses which remain in the church be veiled.

42   Vespers (Evening Prayer) is not celebrated by those who have attended the Mass of the Lord's Supper.

43   The faithful are invited to continue adoration before the Blessed Sacrament for a suitable length of time during the night, according to local circumstances, but after midnight the adoration should take place without solemnity.

44   If the celebration of the Passion of the Lord on the following Friday does not take place in the same church, the Mass is concluded in the usual way and the Blessed Sacrament is placed in the tabernacle.

Reflection

The object of the Triduum is the paschal mystery and not the veneration of the Eucharist. And the primary purpose of the Eucharist is, in turn, food to be shared. Nonetheless, the reservation of the Eucharist for our prayer and meditation is one of the Church's most precious traditions. Furthermore, we must never forget that adoration of the reserved Eucharist is never to be divorced from the Eucharistic sacrifice itself since the former flows from the latter. To quote Pope Paul VI: "The reason adorers continue worship of the Eucharist outside Mass is that they may more fully share in the effects of the sacrifice and be empowered to take part in it more effectively . . ." To spend time in prayer before the Eucharist is certainly one of the best ways to prepare for Good Friday.

Suggested Questions for Discussion

1   What is the purpose of having a solemn procession of the Eucharist on this day?

2   Who should take part in the procession?

3   What factors would influence the choice of a hymn during the procession?

4   What is meant by no "solemn" adoration after midnight?

5   What can be done to facilitate personal prayer during the time of adoration?

FRIDAY OF THE PASSION OF THE LORD (GOOD FRIDAY)

Friday of the Passion of the Lord (Good Friday)

Prayer

LITURGY OF THE WORD
First Reading
Psalm Response
Second Reading
Gospel Acclamation
Passion
Homily
General Intercessions

ADORATION OF THE HOLY CROSS
Showing of the Holy Cross
Veneration of the Holy Cross

HOLY COMMUNION
Prayer over the People

Introduction

Historical Survey

Throughout history the day commemorating the death of Christ has been known by various names. It has been called the "Friday of the Passion and Death of the Lord," the "Friday of *Parasceve*" (or Preparation, from the Jewish day of preparation for the great Sabbath); the Greek Church calls it the "Great Friday"; St. Ambrose (c. 339–397) spoke of it as the "day of sorrow" (expressed by fasting). Today's *Missal* calls it the "Friday of the Passion of the Lord." As to the designation of "Good Friday," some believe that the term was originally "God's Friday" — in the old German phrase *Gute Freitag*, the word *Gute* was an archaic form for *Gott* (God).

Originally no liturgical services were held on this day. People were to fast and do so in a very strict manner. Food and drink were not permitted, although sick people and pregnant women were allowed bread and water. The character of the fast was one of grieving, since the disciples would fast in the absence of the bridegroom (see Mt 9:15; Mk 2:20; Lk 5:34–35). So deeply imbedded was this fast in the piety of the people that Pope Innocent I at the beginning of the fifth century could say, and no one contradicted him, that the apostles themselves observed this practice.

Yet already a century earlier the Christians in Jerusalem began to hold assemblies on Friday. Early in the morning they gathered at Golgotha, this being the beginnings of having the Easter Vigil commemorate the resurrection alone. In the church on Golgotha was a reliquary containing a part of the cross; the bishop presented this relic for the people's veneration. Later in the day, from noon to three in the afternoon, the faithful gathered for a Scripture service with readings (including the Passion account), prayers, and psalms.

It was this sequence of ceremonies which, through the pilgrims returning from Jerusalem to the west, impacted the observance of this day in Europe. In seventh-century Rome, for example, the pope at two in the afternoon left his apartments and carried a relic of the cross as he processed to the Church of the Holy Cross. There the cross was venerated, the Scriptures (including John's account of the Passion) were read, and a series of solemn prayers were said. In time the liturgical structure became: 1. readings followed by solemn prayers; 2. veneration of the cross; and eventually 3. a communion service.

The Good Friday liturgy continued to be celebrated in the afternoon till the fifteenth century when it was moved to the morning. Filling the gap from noon till three o'clock was a three-hour, non-liturgical service, promoted by the Jesuits and originating in South America, consisting of prayers, sermons (often based on the seven last words of Christ), and singing. It was called the *Tre Ore* and filled a spiritual void experienced by most of the faithful who were unable to attend the morning liturgy. Since 1955 the Good Friday liturgy has been restored to the afternoon and is to begin at about "three o'clock (unless a later hour is chosen for a pastoral reason)." (*Roman Missal*)

Documentation

General Instruction of the Liturgy of the Hours

209 Those who take part in . . . the celebration of the Lord's passion on Good Friday do not say evening prayer on [this] day.

Constitution on the Sacred Liturgy

110 Let the paschal fast be kept sacred. Let it be observed everywhere on Good Friday . . . as a way of coming to the joys of the Sunday of the resurrection with uplifted and welcoming heart.

Circular Letter "Paschalis sollemnitatis"

39 The Easter fast is sacred on the first two days of the Triduum, in which, according to ancient tradition, the Church fasts "because the Spouse has been taken away." Good Friday is a day of fasting and abstinence; it is also recommended that Holy Saturday be so observed, so that the Church, with uplifted and welcoming heart, be ready to celebrate the joys of the Sunday of the Resurrection.

40 It is recommended that there be a communal celebration of the Office of Readings and Morning Prayer on Good Friday and Holy Saturday. It is fitting that the bishop should celebrate the Office in the cathedral with, as far as possible, the participation of the clergy and people.

This Office, formerly called "Tenebrae," held a special place in the devotion of the faithful as they meditated upon the passion, death and burial of the Lord, while awaiting the announcement of the resurrection.

V. Good Friday

58 On this day, when "Christ our passover was sacrificed," the Church meditates on the passion of her Lord and Spouse, adores the cross,

commemorates her origin from the side of Christ asleep on the cross, and intercedes for the salvation of the whole world.

59 On this day, in accordance with ancient tradition, the Church does not celebrate the Eucharist: Holy Communion is distributed to the faithful during the Celebration of the Lord's Passion alone, though it may be brought at any time of the day to the sick who cannot take part in the celebration.

60 Good Friday is a day of penance to be observed as an obligation in the whole Church, and indeed, through abstinence and fasting.

61 All celebration of the sacraments on this day is strictly prohibited, except for the sacraments of penance and anointing of the sick. Funerals are to be celebrated without singing, music, or the tolling of bells.

62 It is recommended that on this day the Office of Readings and Morning Prayer be celebrated with the participation of the people in the churches (cf. n. 40).

63 The Celebration of the Lord's passion is to take place in the afternoon, at about three o'clock. The time will be chosen which seems most appropriate for pastoral reasons in order to allow the people to assemble more easily, for example, shortly after midday or in the late evening, however not later than nine o'clock.

64 The Order for the Celebration of the Lord's passion (the liturgy of the word, the adoration of the cross, and Holy Communion), that stems from an ancient tradition of the Church, should be observed faithfully and religiously and may not be changed by anyone on his own initiative.

72 Devotions such as the "Way of the Cross," processions of the passion, and commemorations of the sorrows of the Blessed Virgin Mary are not, for pastoral reasons, to be neglected. The texts and songs used, however, should be adapted to the spirit of the liturgy of this day. Such devotions should be assigned to a time of day that makes it quite clear that the liturgical celebration, by its very nature, far surpasses them in importance.

National Statutes for the Catechumenate

15 Candidates for initiation, as well as those who assist them and participate in the celebration of the Easter Vigil with them, are encouraged to keep and extend the paschal fast of Good Friday, as determined by canon

1251, throughout the day of Holy Saturday until the end of the Vigil itself, in accord with the Constitution on the Liturgy, *Sacrosanctum Concilium*, art. 110.

Roman Missal

First Part:
The Liturgy of the Word

1   On this and the following day, by a most ancient tradition, the Church does not celebrate the Sacraments at all, except for Penance and the Anointing of the Sick.

2   On this day, Holy Communion is distributed to the faithful only within the celebration of the Lord's Passion; but it may be brought at any hour of the day to the sick who cannot participate in this celebration.

3   The altar should be completely bare: without a cross, without candles and without cloths.

4   On the afternoon of this day, about three o'clock (unless a later hour is chosen for a pastoral reason), there takes place the celebration of the Lord's Passion consisting of three parts, namely, the Liturgy of the Word, the Adoration of the Cross, and Holy Communion.

     In the United States, if the size or nature of a parish or other community indicates the pastoral need for an additional liturgical service, the Diocesan Bishop may permit the service to be repeated later. This liturgy by its very nature may not, however, be celebrated in the absence of a Priest.

Reflection

To be sure, there are elements of sadness connected with today's liturgy, and yet what we celebrate is not a funeral. Certainly we recall the death of Jesus, but today is also a day of hope and expectation for we focus not only on Calvary but also, and more importantly, on the whole mystery of our redemption. In the words of Pope Leo the Great: The cross is "the source of every blessing and grace" (Homily on the Passion 8, 6–7). On Good Friday "Christ became our paschal sacrifice," and by so doing leads all of us to his resurrection from the dead. The truth is simple: by dying Christ won for us new life. The structure of the liturgy also is simple. It is ancient and classic.

Suggested Questions for Discussion

1   What feeling(s) should a person experience upon entering the church for today's liturgy?

2   What is the high point of today's liturgy?

3   What factors would enter into a decision as to the time of day for the Good Friday liturgy to be celebrated?

4   How much explanation is necessary to help people understand the structure and meaning of today's liturgy?

5   How important is the paschal fast to the celebration of the Good Friday liturgy?

6   Why are restrictions placed on the number of sacraments that may be celebrated today?

Bibliography

- "Good Friday Reproaches." *BCL Newsletter* 14:2 (February 1978).

- "Good Friday 'Reproaches' (Improperia)." *BCL Newsletter* 16:3 (March 1980).

- "Good Friday Reproaches." *BCL Newsletter* 17:1 (January 1981).

- "Holy Thursday and Good Friday and the Missale Romanum." *BCL Newsletter* 39 (March/April 2003).

- "Proclamation of the Passion in Parts." *BCL Newsletter* 3 (January/February 1999).

- "The Jews and the Passion Narratives in Holy Week." *BCL Newsletter* 43 (February/March 2007).

- Buxton, R.F. "Good Friday." In *The New Westminster Dictionary of Liturgy and Worship*, ed. J.G. Davies. Philadelphia: The Westminster Press, 1986. 251–253.

- Fragomeni, Richard. "Corpus and Cross: Drama and Devotion in the Good Friday Liturgy." *Assembly* 18:1 (January 1992), 544–545, 548.

- Maier, Zita. "Symbol for the Church: Cross or Crucifix." *National Bulletin on Liturgy* 28:140 (Spring 1995), 22-36.

- Regan, Patrick. "Restoring the Cross to Good Friday." *Liturgy* 1:1 (1980), 55–59.

- Regan, Patrick. "Veneration of the Cross." *Worship* 52:1 (January 1978), 2–13.

- Schoenbachler, Tim. "Some Alternate Suggestions: Good Friday & Holy Saturday." *Pastoral Music* 14:3 (February-March 1990), 39–42.

- Wozniak, Robert P. "The Passion of Jesus." *Liturgy* 24:2 (March-April 1979), 37-40.

Good Friday Opening Rite

Historical Survey

The very simplicity of Good Friday's opening rite takes us back to the origins of today's observance. According to its earliest descriptions the Good Friday papal liturgy at Rome began in almost the same manner as the celebration begins today. The pope and his assistants prostrated themselves (a gesture taken from Byzantine court ceremonial and today seen as a sign "of both 'our earthly nature' and of the mourning and grief of the Church") as they prayed silently. Then they rose, kissed the altar and immediately began the service. Today, however, the priest also sets the tone for the service by saying or singing an initial prayer.

Documentation

Circular Letter "Paschalis sollemnitatis"

65   The priest and ministers proceed to the altar in silence, without any singing. If any words of introduction are to be said, they should be pronounced before the ministers enter.

The priest and ministers make a reverence to the altar prostrating themselves. This act of prostration, which is proper to the rite of the day, should be strictly observed for it signifies both the abasement of "earthly man," and also the grief and sorrow of the Church.

As the ministers enter, the faithful should be standing, and thereafter should kneel in silent prayer.

Roman Missal

5   The Priest and the Deacon, if a Deacon is present, wearing red vestments as for Mass, go to the altar in silence and, after making a reverence to the altar, prostrate themselves or, if appropriate, kneel and pray in silence for a while. All others kneel.

6   Then the Priest, with the ministers, goes to the chair where, facing the people, who are standing, he says, with hands extended, one of the following prayers, omitting the invitation *Let us pray.*

Prayer
Remember your mercies, O Lord,
and with your eternal protection sanctify your servants,
for whom Christ your Son,
by the shedding of his Blood,
established the Paschal Mystery.
Who lives and reigns for ever and ever.
R. Amen.
Or:
O God, who by the Passion of Christ your Son, our Lord,
abolished the death inherited from ancient sin
by every succeeding generation,
grant that just as, being conformed to him,
we have borne by the law of nature
the image of the man of earth,
so by the sanctification of grace
we may bear the image of the Man of heaven.
Through Christ our Lord.

Reflection

The very absence of a solemn opening procession, of a greeting and response, of a penitential rite, of the Glory to God — all tell us that this day is unique in the Christian liturgical calendar. We are reminded of a liturgical adage that the most ancient liturgical practices are retained on the most solemn observances of the year. Today is unlike any other day in the year. Certainly there is a note of sadness, but it is also a day for hope, a day for remembering that it is through the paschal mystery in its totality that we join Christ in conquering death and in gaining life anew.

Suggested Questions for Discussion

1   Should the opening procession be practiced?

2   Who should take part in the procession?

3   What type of reverence is made when the ministers reach the sanctuary?

4   Which is more appropriate for your community, singing or reciting the opening prayer?

Liturgy of the Word – Readings/Homily

Historical Survey

Many liturgical historians believe that in its early days the Roman Rite had three readings, a practice that eventually fell out of use till restored on Sundays and feasts by the reform of the Second Vatican Council. And yet during the Good Friday liturgy three readings have always been proclaimed, a sign of the antiquity of this observance.

For centuries the word service began with Hosea 6:1–6, a text especially suitable with its words

"He will revive us after two days;
on the third day he will raise us up,
to live in his presence."

Today, however, the reading is Isaiah 52:13–53:12, the "Fourth Song of the Servant of the LORD."

The second reading is a long-standing selection for this day, namely, Hebrews 4:14–16; 5:7–9, which speaks of Jesus as the "Son of God".

Early on in the development of Good Friday a harmonized account, taken from all four gospels, was read in some localities, but it was John's version that became traditional. During the Middle Ages the text, either all or part of the narrative, was sung in plainsong by three singers, often two deacons in addition to the bishop or priest celebrant. The part of Christ was sung in a low range, slowly and solemnly, that of the narrator in the middle register, and that of the crowd in a high register. Designating the parts were the signs † (Christ), C (*Chronista* or narrator), and S (*Synagogus* or crowd). Eventually the crowd parts could be sung by the choir.

Today the Passion account may be proclaimed by lay readers, with the part of Christ reserved to the priest whenever possible. The Vatican has published a *Passionale* (with each gospel text in Latin and having two melodies), and yet today it is customary to proclaim rather than to sing the Scriptures. Furthermore, the Passion is not a dramatic representation but a solemn although simple proclamation.

Neither incense nor candles are used; there is no greeting or initial sign of the cross.

Documentation

Roman Missal

7   Then all sit and the First Reading, from the Book of the Prophet Isaiah (52: 13-53: 12) is read with its Psalm.

8   The Second Reading, from the Letter to the Hebrews (4: 14-16; 5: 7-9), follows, and then the chant before the Gospel.

9   Then the narrative of the Lord's Passion according to John (18: 1-19: 42) is read in the same way as on the preceding Sunday.

10   After the reading of the Lord's Passion, the Priest gives a brief homily and, at its end, the faithful may be invited to spend a short time in prayer.

Lectionary for Mass

40   Good Friday of the Lord's Passion   A B C

First Reading
He himself was wounded for our sins.
(Fourth oracle of the Servant of the Lord).
A reading from the Book of the Prophet Isaiah   52:13–53:12

See, my servant shall prosper,
he shall be raised high and greatly exalted.
Even as many were amazed at him—
so marred was his look beyond human semblance
and his appearance beyond that of the sons of man—
so shall he startle many nations,
because of him kings shall stand speechless;
for those who have not been told shall see,
those who have not heard shall ponder it.

Who would believe what we have heard?
To whom has the arm of the LORD been revealed?
He grew up like a sapling before him,
like a shoot from the parched earth;
there was in him no stately bearing to make us look at him,
nor appearance that would attract us to him.
He was spurned and avoided by people,
a man of suffering, accustomed to infirmity,
one of those from whom people hide their faces, spurned,
and we held him in no esteem.

Yet it was our infirmities that he bore,
our sufferings that he endured,
while we thought of him as stricken,
as one smitten by God and afflicted.
But he was pierced for our offenses,
crushed for our sins;
upon him was the chastisement that makes us whole,
by his stripes we were healed.
We had all gone astray like sheep,
each following his own way;
but the LORD laid upon him the guilt of us all.

Though he was harshly treated,
he submitted and opened not his mouth;
like a lamb led to the slaughter
or a sheep before the shearers,
he was silent and opened not his mouth.
Oppressed and condemned, he was taken away,
and who would have thought any more of his destiny?
When he was cut off from the land of the living,
and smitten for the sin of his people,
a grave was assigned him among the wicked
and a burial place with evildoers,
though he had done no wrong
nor spoken any falsehood.
But the LORD was pleased
to crush him in infirmity.

If he gives his life as an offering for sin,
he shall see his descendants in a long life,
and the will of the LORD shall be accomplished through him.

Because of his affliction
he shall see the light in fullness of days;
through his suffering, my servant shall justify many,
and their guilt he shall bear.
Therefore I will give him his portion among the great,
and he shall divide the spoils with the mighty,
because he surrendered himself to death
and was counted among the wicked;
and he shall take away the sins of many,
and win pardon for their offenses.

The word of the Lord.

Responsorial Psalm   Ps 31:2, 6, 12–13, 15–16, 17, 25
R. (Lk 23:46) Father, into your hands I commend my spirit.

In you, O LORD, I take refuge;
let me never be put to shame.
In your justice rescue me.
Into your hands I commend my spirit;
you will redeem me, O LORD, O faithful God.
R. Father, into your hands I commend my spirit.

For all my foes I am an object of reproach,
a laughingstock to my neighbors, and a dread to my friends;
they who see me abroad flee from me.
I am forgotten like the unremembered dead;
I am like a dish that is broken.
R. Father, into your hands I commend my spirit.

But my trust is in you, O LORD;
I say, "You are my God.
In your hands is my destiny; rescue me
from the clutches of my enemies and my persecutors."
R. Father, into your hands I commend my spirit.

Let your face shine upon your servant;
save me in your kindness.
Take courage and be stouthearted,
all you who hope in the LORD.
R. Father, into your hands I commend my spirit.

Second Reading

*Jesus learned obedience and became the source of salvation
for all who obey him.*

A reading from the Letter to the Hebrews   4:14–16; 5:7–9

Brothers and sisters:
Since we have a great high priest who has passed through the heavens,
Jesus, the Son of God,
let us hold fast to our confession.
For we do not have a high priest
who is unable to sympathize with our weaknesses,
but one who has similarly been tested in every way,
yet without sin.
So let us confidently approach the throne of grace
to receive mercy and to find grace for timely help.
In the days when Christ was in the flesh,
he offered prayers and supplications with loud cries and tears
to the one who was able to save him from death,
and he was heard because of his reverence.
Son though he was, he learned obedience from what he suffered;
and when he was made perfect,

he became the source of eternal salvation for all who obey him.
The word of the Lord.

Verse before the Gospel
Phil 2:8–9

Christ became obedient to the point of death,
even death on a cross.
Because of this, God greatly exalted him
and bestowed on him the name which is above every other name.

Gospel

The Passion of our Lord Jesus Christ.
The Passion of our Lord Jesus Christ according to John
18:1–19:42

Jesus went out with his disciples across the Kidron valley
to where there was a garden,
into which he and his disciples entered.
Judas his betrayer also knew the place,
because Jesus had often met there with his disciples.
So Judas got a band of soldiers and guards
from the chief priests and the Pharisees
and went there with lanterns, torches, and weapons.
Jesus, knowing everything that was going to happen to him,
went out and said to them, "Whom are you looking for?"
They answered him, "Jesus the Nazorean."
He said to them, "I AM."
Judas his betrayer was also with them.
When he said to them, "I AM, "
they turned away and fell to the ground.
So he again asked them,
"Whom are you looking for?"
They said, "Jesus the Nazorean."
Jesus answered,
"I told you that I AM.
So if you are looking for me, let these men go."
This was to fulfill what he had said,
"I have not lost any of those you gave me."
Then Simon Peter, who had a sword, drew it,
struck the high priest's slave, and cut off his right ear.
The slave's name was Malchus.
Jesus said to Peter,
"Put your sword into its scabbard.
Shall I not drink the cup that the Father gave me?"

So the band of soldiers, the tribune, and the Jewish guards seized Jesus,
bound him, and brought him to Annas first.
He was the father-in-law of Caiaphas,
who was high priest that year.
It was Caiaphas who had counseled the Jews

that it was better that one man should die rather than the people.

Simon Peter and another disciple followed Jesus.
Now the other disciple was known to the high priest,
and he entered the courtyard of the high priest with Jesus.
But Peter stood at the gate outside.
So the other disciple, the acquaintance of the high priest,
went out and spoke to the gatekeeper and brought Peter in.
Then the maid who was the gatekeeper said to Peter,
"You are not one of this man's disciples, are you?"
He said, "I am not."
Now the slaves and the guards were standing around a charcoal fire
that they had made, because it was cold,
and were warming themselves.
Peter was also standing there keeping warm.

The high priest questioned Jesus
about his disciples and about his doctrine.
Jesus answered him,
"I have spoken publicly to the world.
I have always taught in a synagogue
or in the temple area where all the Jews gather,
and in secret I have said nothing. Why ask me?
Ask those who heard me what I said to them.
They know what I said."
When he had said this,
one of the temple guards standing there struck Jesus and said,
"Is this the way you answer the high priest?"
Jesus answered him,
"If I have spoken wrongly, testify to the wrong;
but if I have spoken rightly, why do you strike me?"
Then Annas sent him bound to Caiaphas the high priest.

Now Simon Peter was standing there keeping warm.
And they said to him,
"You are not one of his disciples, are you?"
He denied it and said,
"I am not."
One of the slaves of the high priest,
a relative of the one whose ear Peter had cut off, said,
"Didn't I see you in the garden with him?"
Again Peter denied it.
And immediately the cock crowed.

Then they brought Jesus from Caiaphas to the praetorium.
It was morning.
And they themselves did not enter the praetorium,
in order not to be defiled so that they could eat the Passover.

So Pilate came out to them and said,
"What charge do you bring against this man?"
They answered and said to him,
"If he were not a criminal,
we would not have handed him over to you."
At this, Pilate said to them,
"Take him yourselves, and judge him according to your law."
The Jews answered him,
"We do not have the right to execute anyone, "
in order that the word of Jesus might be fulfilled
that he said indicating the kind of death he would die.
So Pilate went back into the praetorium
and summoned Jesus and said to him,
"Are you the King of the Jews?"
Jesus answered,
"Do you say this on your own
or have others told you about me?"
Pilate answered,
"I am not a Jew, am I?
Your own nation and the chief priests handed you over to me.
What have you done?"
Jesus answered,
"My kingdom does not belong to this world.
If my kingdom did belong to this world,
my attendants would be fighting
to keep me from being handed over to the Jews.
But as it is, my kingdom is not here."
So Pilate said to him,
"Then you are a king?"
Jesus answered,
"You say I am a king.
For this I was born and for this I came into the world,
to testify to the truth.
Everyone who belongs to the truth listens to my voice."
Pilate said to him, "What is truth?"

When he had said this,
he again went out to the Jews and said to them,
"I find no guilt in him.
But you have a custom that I release one prisoner to you at Passover.
Do you want me to release to you the King of the Jews?"
They cried out again,
"Not this one but Barabbas!"
Now Barabbas was a revolutionary.

Then Pilate took Jesus and had him scourged.
And the soldiers wove a crown out of thorns and placed it on his head,
  and clothed him in a purple cloak,

and they came to him and said,
"Hail, King of the Jews!"
And they struck him repeatedly.
Once more Pilate went out and said to them,
"Look, I am bringing him out to you,
so that you may know that I find no guilt in him."
So Jesus came out,
wearing the crown of thorns and the purple cloak.
And he said to them, "Behold, the man!"
When the chief priests and the guards saw him they cried out,
"Crucify him, crucify him!"
Pilate said to them,
"Take him yourselves and crucify him.
I find no guilt in him."
The Jews answered,
"We have a law, and according to that law he ought to die,
because he made himself the Son of God."
Now when Pilate heard this statement, he became even more afraid,
and went back into the praetorium and said to Jesus,
"Where are you from?"
Jesus did not answer him.
So Pilate said to him,
"Do you not speak to me?
Do you not know that I have power to release you
and I have power to crucify you?"
Jesus answered him,
"You would have no power over me
if it had not been given to you from above.
For this reason the one who handed me over to you
has the greater sin."
Consequently, Pilate tried to release him; but the Jews cried out,
"If you release him, you are not a friend of Caesar.
Everyone who makes himself a king opposes Caesar."

When Pilate heard these words he brought Jesus out
and seated him on the judge's bench
in the place called Stone Pavement, in Hebrew, Gabbatha.
It was preparation day for Passover, and it was about noon.
And he said to the Jews,
"Behold, your king!" They cried out,
"Take him away, take him away! Crucify him!"
Pilate said to them,
"Shall I crucify your king?"
The chief priests answered,
"We have no king but Caesar."
Then he handed him over to them to be crucified.

So they took Jesus, and, carrying the cross himself,
he went out to what is called the Place of the Skull,
in Hebrew, Golgotha.
There they crucified him, and with him two others,
one on either side, with Jesus in the middle.
Pilate also had an inscription written and put on the cross.
It read,
"Jesus the Nazorean, the King of the Jews."
Now many of the Jews read this inscription,
because the place where Jesus was crucified was near the city;
and it was written in Hebrew, Latin, and Greek.
So the chief priests of the Jews said to Pilate,
"Do not write 'The King of the Jews,'
but that he said, 'I am the King of the Jews'."
Pilate answered,
"What I have written, I have written."

When the soldiers had crucified Jesus,
they took his clothes and divided them into four shares,
a share for each soldier.
They also took his tunic, but the tunic was seamless,
woven in one piece from the top down.
So they said to one another,
"Let's not tear it, but cast lots for it to see whose it will be, "
in order that the passage of Scripture might be fulfilled that says:
They divided my garments among them,
and for my vesture they cast lots.
This is what the soldiers did.
Standing by the cross of Jesus were his mother
and his mother's sister, Mary the wife of Clopas,
and Mary of Magdala.
When Jesus saw his mother and the disciple there whom he loved
he said to his mother, "Woman, behold, your son."
Then he said to the disciple,
"Behold, your mother."
And from that hour the disciple took her into his home.

After this, aware that everything was now finished,
in order that the Scripture might be fulfilled,
Jesus said, "I thirst."
There was a vessel filled with common wine.
So they put a sponge soaked in wine on a sprig of hyssop
and put it up to his mouth.
When Jesus had taken the wine, he said,
"It is finished."
And bowing his head, he handed over the spirit.

(Here all kneel and pause for a short time.)

Now since it was preparation day,
in order that the bodies might not remain
on the cross on the sabbath,
for the sabbath day of that week was a solemn one,
the Jews asked Pilate that their legs be broken
and that they be taken down.
So the soldiers came and broke the legs of the first
and then of the other one who was crucified with Jesus.
But when they came to Jesus and saw that he was already dead,
they did not break his legs,
but one soldier thrust his lance into his side,
and immediately blood and water flowed out.
An eyewitness has testified, and his testimony is true;
he knows that he is speaking the truth,
so that you also may come to believe.
For this happened so that the Scripture passage might be fulfilled:
Not a bone of it will be broken.
And again another passage says:
They will look upon him whom they have pierced.

After this, Joseph of Arimathea,
secretly a disciple of Jesus for fear of the Jews,
asked Pilate if he could remove the body of Jesus.
And Pilate permitted it.
So he came and took his body.
Nicodemus, the one who had first come to him at night,
also came bringing a mixture of myrrh and aloes
weighing about one hundred pounds.
They took the body of Jesus
and bound it with burial cloths along with the spices,
according to the Jewish burial custom.
Now in the place where he had been crucified there was a garden,
and in the garden a new tomb, in which no one had yet been buried.
So they laid Jesus there because of the Jewish preparation day;
for the tomb was close by.

The Gospel of the Lord.

Reflection

Today's readings present us with a rich mosaic of biblical images. Jesus is the suffering servant (first reading), the lamb led to slaughter, the great high priest (second reading), the exalted one, the king of the Jews. Each image contributes to our understanding of his mission on our behalf. Each image opens another door through which we can pass to join Christ in his passage through death to a new and victorious life.

Suggested Questions for Discussion

1   Who may preside at the reading of the Passion?

2   Why is the Passion proclaimed without candles, greeting, or sign of the cross?

3   In some parishes the people sit during the Passion. Good idea?

4   What are the weaknesses, if any, of having the assembly take the part of the mob, e.g., by shouting "Crucify him . . ."

5   How can funeral imagery be avoided during the proclamation of the Passion?

6   In the homily what references, if any, should be made to the Jewish people?

Liturgy of the Word – Solemn Prayers

Historical Survey

The solemn prayers represent the most ancient form of what we today know as the Prayer of the Faithful (restored by the Second Vatican Council). Somewhat early on in western liturgical history this series of petitionary prayer fell out of use in Rome, being retained only on the most solemn day of Good Friday and with a text going back to an early period of liturgical history.

The structure of the solemn prayers is three-fold: the presiding minister announces an intention; the deacon calls for silent prayer or for all to kneel while praying silently; and then the presider sums up and vocalizes the unspoken prayer of all.

The earliest series of these Good Friday prayers included nine petitions: for the Church, the pope, the clergy and laity, the king, those preparing for Baptism, the needs of the faithful, heretics and schismatics, the Jewish people, and pagans. The petition for the Jewish people spoke of the "*perfidis iudaeis,*" and whereas the people knelt while praying for other intentions, they did not do so when praying for the Jews. Religious writers, when commenting on this manifestation of anti-Semitism, would say that "the Roman soldiers bowed down their knees before Jesus in mock adoration during the Passion, and that the chief priests together with the scribes mocked him."

Although the solemn prayers are an ancient element in the Good Friday liturgy, their recent history evidences change and evolution. Two of the prayers have been rewritten, namely, that for the Jews and that for heretics and schismatics. A new prayer, for those who do not believe in Christ, has been added, apparently due to recent Roman contacts and dialogue with Muslims. And after the first three intentions (Church, pope, clergy and laity) the order of the petitions has been altered.

Documentation

Ecumenical Directory

22   It is fitting that prayers for unity be offered regularly at special times, such as: . . . Good Friday . . . commemorating the mystery of the cross, which gathers together the scattered children of God.

Circular Letter "Paschalis sollemnitatis"

67   The General Intercessions are to follow the wording and form handed down by ancient tradition maintaining the full range of intentions so as to signify clearly the universal effect of the passion of Christ, who hung on the cross for the salvation of the whole world. In case of grave public necessity the local Ordinary may permit or prescribe the adding of special intentions.

In this event the priest is permitted to select from the prayers of the Missal those more appropriate to local circumstances, in such a way however that the series follows the rule for General Intercessions.

Roman Missal

The Solemn Intercessions

11   The Liturgy of the Word concludes with the Solemn Intercessions, which take place in this way: the Deacon, if a Deacon is present, or if he is not, a lay minister, stands at the ambo, and sings or says the invitation in which the intention is expressed. Then all pray in silence for a while, and afterwards the Priest, standing at the chair or, if appropriate, at the altar, with hands extended, sings or says the prayer.

The faithful may remain either kneeling or standing throughout the entire period of the prayers.

12 Before the Priest's prayer, in accord with tradition, it is permissible to use the Deacon's invitations *Let us kneel—let us stand*, with all kneeling for silent prayer.

The Conferences of Bishops may provide other invitations to introduce the prayer of the Priest.

13 In a situation of grave public need, the Diocesan Bishop may permit or order the addition of a special intention.

I.   For Holy Church
Let us pray, dearly beloved, for the holy Church of God,
that our God and Lord be pleased to give her peace,
to guard her and to unite her throughout the whole world
and grant that, leading our life in tranquility and quiet,
we may glorify God the Father almighty.
Prayer in silence. Then the Priest says:
Almighty ever-living God,
who in Christ revealed your glory to all the nations,
watch over the works of your mercy,
that your Church, spread throughout all the world,
may persevere with steadfast faith in confessing your name.
Through Christ our Lord.
R. Amen.

II.   For the Pope
Let us pray also for our most Holy Father Pope *N.*,
that our God and Lord,
who chose him for the Order of Bishops,
may keep him safe and unharmed for the Lord's holy Church,
to govern the holy People of God.
Prayer in silence. Then the Priest says.
Almighty ever-living God,
by whose decree all things are founded,
look with favor on our prayers
and in your kindness protect the Pope chosen for us,
that, under him, the Christian people,
governed by you their maker,
may grow in merit by reason of their faith.
Through Christ our Lord.
R. Amen.

III.   For all orders and degrees of the faithful
Let us pray also for our bishop, *N.*,

for all Bishops, Priests, and Deacons of the Church
and for the whole of the faithful people.
Prayer in silence. Then the Priest says.
Almighty ever-living God,
by whose Spirit the whole body of the Church
is sanctified and governed,
hear our humble prayer for your ministers,
that, by the gift of your grace,
all may serve you faithfully.
Through Christ our Lord.
R. Amen.

IV.   For catechumens

Let us pray also for (our) catechumens,
that our God and Lord
may open wide the ears of their inmost hearts
and unlock the gates of his mercy,
that, having received forgiveness of all their sins
through the waters of rebirth,
they, too, may be one with Christ Jesus our Lord.
Prayer in silence. Then the Priest says.
Almighty ever-living God,
who make your Church ever fruitful with new offspring,
increase the faith and understanding of (our) catechumens,
that, reborn in the font of Baptism,
they may be added to the number of your adopted children.
Through Christ our Lord.
R. Amen.

V.   For the unity of Christians

Let us pray also for all our brothers and sisters who believe in Christ,
that our God and Lord may be pleased,
as they live the truth,
to gather them together and keep them in his one Church.
Prayer in silence. Then the Priest says.
Almighty ever-living God,
who gather what is scattered
and keep together what you have gathered,
look kindly on the flock of your Son,
that those whom one Baptism has consecrated
may be joined together by integrity of faith
and united in the bond of charity.
Through Christ our Lord.
R. Amen.

VI.   For the Jewish people

Let us pray also for the Jewish people,
to whom the Lord our God spoke first,

that he may grant them to advance in love of his name
and in faithfulness to his covenant.
Prayer in silence. Then the Priest says.
Almighty ever-living God,
who bestowed your promises on Abraham and his descendants,
graciously hear the prayers of your Church,
that the people you first made your own
may attain the fullness of redemption.
Through Christ our Lord.
R. Amen.

VII. For those who do not believe in Christ
Let us pray also for those who do not believe in Christ,
that, enlightened by the Holy Spirit,
they, too, may enter on the way of salvation.
Prayer in silence. Then the Priest says.
Almighty ever-living God,
grant to those who do not confess Christ
that, by walking before you with a sincere heart,
they may find the truth
and that we ourselves, being constant in mutual love
and striving to understand more fully the mystery of your life,
may be made more perfect witnesses to your love in the world.
Through Christ our Lord.
R. Amen.

VIII. For those who do not believe in God
Let us pray also for those who do not acknowledge God,
that, following what is right in sincerity of heart,
they may find the way to God himself.
Prayer in silence. Then the Priest says.
Almighty ever-living God,
who created all people
to seek you always by desiring you
and, by finding you, come to rest,
grant, we pray,
that, despite every harmful obstacle,
all may recognize the signs of your fatherly love
and the witness of the good works
done by those who believe in you,
and so in gladness confess you,
the one true God and Father of our human race.
Through Christ our Lord.
R. Amen.

IX. For those in public office
Let us pray also for those in public office,
that our God and Lord

may direct their minds and hearts according to his will
for the true peace and freedom of all.
Prayer in silence. Then the Priest says.
Almighty ever-living God,
in whose hand lies every human heart
and the rights of peoples,
look with favor, we pray,
on those who govern with authority over us,
that throughout the whole world,
the prosperity of peoples,
the assurance of peace,
and freedom of religion
may through your gift be made secure.
Through Christ our Lord.
R. Amen.

X.   For those in tribulation
Let us pray, dearly beloved,
to God the Father almighty,
that he may cleanse the world of all errors,
banish disease, drive out hunger,
unlock prisons, loosen fetters,
granting to travelers safety, to pilgrims return,
health to the sick, and salvation to the dying.
Prayer in silence. Then the Priest says.
Almighty ever-living God,
comfort of mourners, strength of all who toil,
may the prayers of those who cry out in any tribulation
come before you,
that all may rejoice,
because in their hour of need
your mercy was at hand.
Through Christ our Lord.
R. Amen.

Reflection

Although there is nothing in the solemn prayers, which someone has called "con-celebrated" prayers, that explicitly relates to the events of Good Friday, it is with good reason that the Church continues this ancient tradition since the Church, if it is to be faithful to the example of Christ, must be catholic. It must be concerned with both its members and its nonmembers. Just as Jesus on the cross drew all to himself and offered himself for all, so does the Church concern itself with every type of person. The whole assembly is to respond to the New Testament request: "First of all, then, I ask that supplications, prayers, petitions . . . be offered for everyone" (1 Tim 2:1).

Suggested Questions for Discussion

1   How much freedom is allowed as to the literary/musical form of the solemn prayers?

2   How much freedom is allowed as to the posture of the people during these prayers?

3   How does singing add to the solemnity of these prayers?

4   Is it appropriate to sing some of the prayers and recite others?

Adoration of the Holy Cross

Historical Survey

According to a fourth-century tradition it was in 326 that the Empress Helena (c. 255–c. 330), the mother of Constantine the Emperor, discovered the cross upon which Jesus was crucified. At any rate, it was not long before relics believed to have been taken from this cross became objects of piety among the faithful, who paid them special honor on Good Friday.

Egeria, our informative Spanish nun, describes for us what took place in Jerusalem where on Good Friday morning all the people went out to Golgotha. "The bishop sits on his throne, a table covered with linen cloth is set before him, and the deacons stand around the table. The gilded silver casket containing the sacred wood of the cross is brought in and opened. Both the wood of the cross and the inscription are taken out and placed on the table. As soon as they have been placed on the table, the bishop, remaining seated, grips the ends of the sacred wood with his hands, while the deacons, who are standing about, keep watch over it. . . . It is the practice here for all the people to come forth one by one, the faithful as well as the catechumens, to bow down before the table, kiss the holy wood, and then move on. . . . All the people pass through one by one; all of them bow down, touching the cross and the inscription, first with their foreheads, then with their eyes; and, after kissing it, they move on" (Chapter 37).

This ceremony of venerating the cross, traveling from Jerusalem to Rome, took place as follows in the eighth-century papal Good Friday liturgy. About two in the afternoon the pope and his ministers leave the papal apartment. All are barefoot as they move in procession while the psalm *Beati immaculati* is chanted. The archdeacon holds the pope's left hand, and the pope carries a censer in his right hand. Another deacon, behind the pope, carries the wood of the precious cross in a golden reliquary decorated with gems; the cross itself is covered with gold and precious stones. When all arrive at the Church of Jerusalem, they enter, the deacon places the reliquary containing the relic upon the altar, and the pope opens it. Then he prostrates before the altar in order to pray and, when he arises, he kisses the relic, withdraws, and sits in his chair. Upon his order the bishops, priests, deacons, and subdeacons kiss the cross placed on the altar. Then the relic is placed on a small stand at the doors of the chancel, and the rest of those present kiss it. The women, however, do not go within, but afterwards ministers carry it to them to be kissed.

Depending on the locality, the showing of the cross took place at various places within the liturgy, at times at the beginning of the service (the eighth-century papal liturgy), at times before the communion. And yet it was not long till the rite received an expansion. For example, already before 900 in France the cross, held by two acolytes, was covered. Two cantors sang *Agios o theos* to which the choir gave the Latin equivalent *Sanctus Deus*. This refrain-response was repeated three times. Then the bishop uncovered the cross and sang *Ecce lignum crucis*. Afterwards all venerated the cross.

By the twelfth century this unveiling ceremony reached Rome where, now even more dramatic in structure, it entered the pope's liturgy. The pontiff unveiled the cross in three steps, each time singing the *Ecce lignum* followed by its response *Venite, adoremus*.

Today there are two forms for showing the cross to the community. The cross is either unveiled in the sanctuary in three stages, or else an uncovered cross is brought in procession from the church door.

Documentation

Circular Letter "Paschalis sollemnitatis"

68   For veneration of the cross, let a cross be used that is of appropriate size and beauty, and let one of the forms for this rite as found in the Roman Missal be followed. The rite should be carried out with the splendor worthy of the mystery of our salvation: both the invitation pronounced at the unveiling of the cross, and the people's response should be made in song, and a period of respectful silence is to be observed after each act of veneration — the celebrant standing and holding the raised cross.

Second Part:
The Adoration of the Holy Cross

14   After the Solemn Intercessions, the solemn Adoration of the Holy Cross takes place. Of the two forms of the showing of the Cross presented here, the more appropriate one, according to pastoral needs, should be chosen.

The Showing of the Holy Cross (First Form)

15   The Deacon accompanied by ministers, or another suitable minister, goes to the sacristy, from which, in procession, accompanied by two ministers with lighted candles, he carries the Cross, covered with a violet veil, through the church to the middle of the sanctuary

The Priest, standing before the altar and facing the people, receives the Cross, uncovers a little of its upper part and elevates it while beginning the *Ecce lignum Crucis (Behold the wood of the Cross)*. He is assisted in singing by the Deacon or, if need be, by the choir. All respond, *Come, let us adore.* At the end of the singing, all kneel and for a brief moment adore in silence, while the Priest stands and holds the Cross raised
V. Behold the wood of the Cross, on which hung the salvation of the world.
R. Come, let us adore.

Then the Priest uncovers the right arm of the Cross and again, raising up the Cross, begins, *Behold the wood of the Cross* and everything takes place as above.

Finally, he uncovers the Cross entirely and, raising it up, he begins the invitation *Behold the wood of the Cross* a third time and everything takes place like the first time.

The Showing of the Holy Cross (Second Form)

16   The Priest or the Deacon accompanied by ministers, or another suitable minister, goes to the door of the church, where he receives the unveiled Cross, and the ministers take lighted candles; then the procession sets off through the church to the sanctuary, the one who carries the Cross elevates it, singing, *Behold the wood of the Cross,* to which all respond, *Come, let us adore.* After each response all kneel and for a brief moment adore in silence, as above.

The Adoration of the Holy Cross

17   Then, accompanied by two ministers with lighted candles, the Priest or the Deacon carries the Cross to the entrance of the sanctuary or to another

suitable place and there puts it down or hands it over to the ministers to hold. Candles are placed on the right and left sides of the Cross.

Reflection

Within past years many authors have called attention to using a cross and not a crucifix for the Good Friday liturgy, and with good reason. The very origin of the veneration involved wood, wood from the true cross. Just as the wood of a tree brought about the fall in the garden of paradise, so it is that the wood of a tree brings about our salvation; Satan, who conquered through a tree, is overcome by a tree. The object of our attention is the wood of the cross and not the image upon it. It is by no means inconsequential that the official liturgical texts speak of a "cross" and not a "crucifix."

Suggested Questions for Discussion

1   What factors might influence the choice of the manner of showing the cross?

2   How long should the period of silence last?

Veneration of the Holy Cross

Historical Survey

One of the special characteristics of Good Friday is the veneration (adoration) of the cross. After the cross has been laid down or given to ministers to hold, all approach it and perform some sign of reverence. Meanwhile, there is singing.

We do not know whether song originally accompanied this rite, although by the tenth century the liturgical books offered a wide variety of antiphons and other chants from which to choose. Today the *Missal* gives three possibilities: the "*Crucem tuam*"; the reproaches; the hymn "*Pange, lingua*" — all taken from the church's traditional musical repertory.

The "We worship you, Lord" (*Crucem tuam*), having its origins in either Egypt or Byzantium, was already known in France during the early ninth century. The text wonderfully expresses the unity of the Triduum: ". . . we venerate your cross, we praise your resurrection . . ."

The reproaches or *Improperia* consist of a set of reproofs addressed by Jesus to the people. A comparison is made between the divine compassion and the sufferings inflicted upon the speaker, namely, Jesus himself. The reproaches belong to a literary genre often found in Scripture, for example, Deuteronomy 32; Micha 6:3–5; Psalms 77 and 105. At least part of the text, probably of French or Byzantine origin, dates from the eighth century. Since the *Improperia* (really a dialogue between God and the Church today) can be misunderstood, some suggest that this composition not be used.

Each of the first three verses is followed by the *Trisagion* (from the Greek "thrice holy"), which is found in all the ancient eastern liturgies and was inserted into the Roman liturgy at a time when eastern influence was strong in Italy. Each of the other verses, sometimes called the "small *Improperia*" and dating later than the first three verses, is followed by the antiphon "My people . . ."

The *Missal* also suggests the hymn *"Pange, lingua"* — not the well-known eucharistic hymn written by St. Thomas Aquinas (c. 1225–1274) — but rather a passion hymn composed by Venatius Fortunatus (c. 535–c. 600), an Italian who became the bishop of Poitiers. An English translation, "The Royal Banners," extolling the cross, may be found in several worship aids.

Documentation

Circular Letter "Paschalis sollemnitatis"

69   The cross is to be presented to each of the faithful individually for their adoration, since the personal adoration of the cross is a most important feature in this celebration. Only when necessitated by the large numbers of faithful present should the rite of veneration be made simultaneously by all present.

Only one cross should be used for the veneration, as this contributes to the full symbolism of the rite. During the veneration of the cross the antiphons, "Reproaches," and hymns should be sung, so that the history of salvation be commemorated through song. Other appropriate songs may also be sung (cf. n. 42).

Roman Missal

18   For the Adoration of the Cross, first the Priest Celebrant alone approaches, with the chasuble and his shoes removed, if appropriate. Then the clergy, the lay ministers, and the faithful approach, moving as if in procession, and showing reverence to the Cross by a simple genuflec-

tion or by some other sign appropriate to the usage of the region, for example, by kissing the Cross.

19   Only one Cross should be offered for adoration. If, because of the large number of people, it is not possible for all to approach individually, the Priest, after some of the clergy and faithful have adored, takes the Cross and, standing in the middle before the altar, invites the people in a few words to adore the Holy Cross and afterwards holds the Cross elevated higher for a brief time, for the faithful to adore it in silence.

20   While the adoration of the Holy Cross is taking place, the antiphon *Crucem tuam adoramus* (We adore your Cross, O Lord), the Reproaches, the hymn *Crux fidelis* (Faithful Cross) or other suitable chants are sung, during which all who have already adored the Cross remain seated.

Chants to Be Sung during the Adoration of the Holy Cross

Ant. We adore your Cross, O Lord
we praise and glorify your holy Resurrection,
for behold, because of the wood of a tree
joy has come to the whole world.

May God have mercy on us and bless us;   Cf. Ps 67 (66): 2
may he let his face shed its light upon us
and have mercy on us.

Ant. We adore . . .

The Reproaches

Parts assigned to one of the two choirs separately are indicated by the numbers 1 (first choir) and 2 (second choir); parts sung by both choirs together are marked: 1 and 2. Some of the verses may also be sung by two cantors.

I

1 and 2:
My people, what have I done to you?
Or how have I grieved you? Answer me!

1:
Because I led you out of the land of Egypt,
you have prepared a Cross for your Savior.

1: Hagios o Theos,

2: Holy is God,

1: Hagios Ischyros,

2: Holy and Mighty,

1: Hagios Athanatos, eleison himas.

2: Holy and Immortal One, have mercy on us.

1 and 2:
Because I led you out through the desert forty years
and fed you with manna and brought you into a land of plenty,
you have prepared a Cross for your Savior.

1: Hagios o Theos,

2: Holy is God,

1: Hagios Ischyros,

2: Holy and Mighty,

1: Hagios Athanatos, eleison himas.

2: Holy and Immortal One, have mercy on us.

1 and 2:
What more should I have done for you and have not done?
Indeed, I planted you as my most beautiful chosen vine
and you have turned very bitter for me,
for in my thirst you gave me vinegar to drink
and with a lance you pierced your Savior's side.

1: Hagios o Theos,

2: Holy is God,

1: Hagios Ischyros,

2: Holy and Mighty,

1: Hagios Athanatos, eleison himas.

2: Holy and Immortal One, have mercy on us.

II

Cantors:
I scourged Egypt for your sake with its firstborn sons,
and you scourged me and handed me over.

1 and 2 repeat:
My people, what have I done to you?
Or how have I grieved you? Answer me!

Cantors:
I led you out from Egypt as Pharaoh lay sunk in the Red Sea,
and you handed me over to the chief priests.

1 and 2 repeat:
My people, what have I done to you?
Or how have I grieved you? Answer me!

Cantors:
I opened up the sea before you,
and you opened my side with a lance.

1 and 2 repeat:
My people, what have I done to you?
Or how have I grieved you? Answer me!

Cantors:
I went before you in a pillar of cloud,
and you led me into Pilate's palace.

1 and 2 repeat:
My people, what have I done to you?
Or how have I grieved you? Answer me!

Cantors:
I fed you with manna in the desert,
and on me you rained blows and lashes.

1 and 2 repeat:
My people, what have I done to you?
Or how have I grieved you? Answer me!

Cantors:
I gave you saving water from the rock to drink,
and for drink you gave me gall and vinegar.

1 and 2 repeat:
My people, what have I done to you?

Or how have I grieved you? Answer me!

Cantors:
I struck down for you the kings of the Canaanites,
and you struck my head with a reed.

1 and 2 repeat:
My people, what have I done to you?
Or how have I grieved you? Answer me!

Cantors:
I put in your hand a royal scepter,
and you put on my head a crown of thorns.

1 and 2 repeat:
My people, what have I done to you?
Or how have I grieved you? Answer me!

Cantors:
I exalted you with great power,
and you hung me on the scaffold of the Cross.

1 and 2 repeat:
My people, what have I done to you?
Or how have I grieved you? Answer me!

Hymn

All:
Faithful Cross the Saints rely on,
Noble tree beyond compare!
Never was there such a scion,
Never leaf or flower so rare.
Sweet the timber, sweet the iron,
Sweet the burden that they bear!

Cantors:
Sing, my tongue in exultation
Of our banner and device!
Make a solemn proclamation
Of a triumph and its price:
How the Savior of creation
Conquered by his sacrifice!

All:
Faithful Cross the Saints rely on,
Noble tree beyond compare!

Never was there such a scion,
Never leaf or flower so rare.

Cantors:
For, when Adam first offended,
Eating that forbidden fruit,
Not all hopes of glory ended
With the serpent at the root:
Broken nature would be mended
By a second tree and shoot.

All:
Sweet the timber, sweet the iron,
Sweet the burden that they bear!

Cantors:
Thus the tempter was outwitted
By a wisdom deeper still:
Remedy and ailment fitted,
Means to cure and means to kill;
That the world might be acquitted,
Christ would do his Father's will.

All:
Faithful Cross the Saints rely on,
Noble tree beyond compare!
Never was there such a scion,
Never leaf or flower so rare.

Cantors:
So the Father, out of pity
For our self-inflicted doom,
Sent him from the heavenly city
When the holy time had come:
He, the Son and the Almighty,
Took our flesh in Mary's womb.

All:
Sweet the timber, sweet the iron,
Sweet the burden that they bear!

Cantors:
Hear a tiny baby crying,
Founder of the seas and strands;
See his virgin Mother tying
Cloth around his feet and hands;
Find him in a manger lying
Tightly wrapped in swaddling-bands!

All:
Faithful Cross the Saints rely on,
Noble tree beyond compare!
Never was there such a scion,
Never leaf or flower so rare.

Cantors:
So he came, the long-expected,
Not in glory, not to reign;
Only born to be rejected,
Choosing hunger, toil and pain,
Till the scaffold was erected
And the Paschal Lamb was slain.

All:
Sweet the timber, sweet the iron,
Sweet the burden that they bear!

Cantors:
No disgrace was too abhorrent:
Nailed and mocked and parched he died;
Blood and water, double warrant,
Issue from his wounded side,
Washing in a mighty torrent
Earth and stars and oceantide.

All:
Faithful Cross the Saints rely on,
Noble tree beyond compare!
Never was there such a scion,
Never leaf or flower so rare.

Cantors:
Lofty timber, smooth your roughness,
Flex your boughs for blossoming;
Let your fibers lose their toughness,
Gently let your tendrils cling;
Lay aside your native gruffness,
Clasp the body of your King!

All:
Sweet the timber, sweet the iron,
Sweet the burden that they bear!

Cantors:
Noblest tree of all created,
Richly jeweled and embossed:
Post by Lamb's blood consecrated;
Spar that saves the tempest-tossed;

Scaffold-beam which, elevated,
Carries what the world has cost!

All:
Faithful Cross the Saints rely on,
Noble tree beyond compare!
Never was there such a scion,
Never leaf or flower so rare.

The following conclusion is never to be omitted:

All:
Wisdom, power, and adoration
To the blessed Trinity
For redemption and salvation
Through the Paschal Mystery,
Now, in every generation,
And for all eternity. Amen.

In accordance with local circumstances or popular traditions and if it is pastorally appropriate, the *Stabat Mater* may be sung, as found in the *Graduale Romanum*, or another suitable chant in memory of the compassion of the Blessed Virgin Mary.

21   When the adoration has been concluded, the Cross is carried by the Deacon or a minister to its place at the altar. Lighted candles are placed around or on the altar or near the Cross.

Reflection

Our liturgical books have historically referred to the "adoration" of the cross. To be sure, it is God and God alone who is adored: Father, Son, and Holy Spirit. And yet the cross, in the church's tradition, has, so to speak, almost become an essential and intimate part of Christ's victory over death. It is a symbol of our unity as Christians who again and again join in living the Christian mystery.

Suggested Questions for Discussion

1   What various musical options are possible while the people venerate the cross?

2   When should this music begin and conclude?

3   How great a danger is there that the reproaches, if used, might be interpreted in an anti-Semitic manner?

4   Why is it normative that only one cross is to be used for the veneration?

5   What pastoral reasons would justify using a second or third cross?

6   Is the cross placed in such a way that it can be easily venerated by the elderly?

Communion Rite

Historical Survey

The Roman Church has never celebrated Mass on Good Friday, and for centuries communion, which was considered to break the fast before the Vigil, was not distributed on this day. Good Friday was primitively a day of fasting, prayer, and private pious observances, and not one for gathering in liturgical assembly. But once a liturgy came to be celebrated on Friday, the people gradually desired to receive the Eucharist, a sacrament so closely allied with Christ's sacrifice on the cross. Although the papal liturgy (always quite conservative in nature and in this matter following the practice of the East) for some time continued to exclude any reception of communion by the faithful, the people who wanted to receive simply went to their parish churches later in the day for a liturgy during which they received the Eucharist.

But since there was no Mass, it was the consecrated bread and wine reserved overnight from Holy Thursday that was distributed. In time only the consecrated bread was reserved; some of the eucharistic bread was placed in a cup of unconsecrated wine, this wine thus being transformed by coming into contact with the eucharistic bread.

By the thirteenth century it was only the pope who received communion; reception of the Eucharist by the people, other than in Germany and Spain, had generally become rare. At the same time what had been a simple communion rite was somewhat expanded with the recitation of the Our Father and other prayers, this being known as the "Mass of the Presanctified."

When the reform of the Triduum was being discussed, some liturgical scholars wanted the old custom of not receiving the Eucharist retained as a sign of our hungering for the redemption brought about through Christ's dying and rising. However, when the 1955 rites were issued, the people were once again permitted to receive the Eucharist on this day but not during a eucharistic celebration itself. Thus, following the Adoration of the Cross, the celebrant proceeds directly to a modified communion rite. Contrary to ancient tradition, the consecrated wine is not distributed and thus is not reserved from Holy Thursday.

Documentation

Circular Letter "Paschalis sollemnitatis"

70   The priest sings the invitation to the Lord's Prayer which is then sung by all. The sign of peace is not exchanged. The Communion Rite is as described in the Missal.

During the distribution of Communion, Psalm 21 or another suitable song may be sung. When Communion has been distributed the pyx is taken to a place prepared for it outside of the church.

Roman Missal

Third Part:
Holy Communion

22   A cloth is spread on the altar, and a corporal and the Missal put in place. Meanwhile the Deacon or, if there is no Deacon, the Priest himself, putting on a humeral veil, brings the Blessed Sacrament back from the place of repose to the altar by a shorter route, while all stand in silence. Two ministers with lighted candles accompany the Blessed Sacrament and place their candlesticks around or upon the altar.

When the Deacon, if a Deacon is present, has placed the Blessed Sacrament upon the altar and uncovered the ciborium, the Priest goes to the altar and genuflects.

23   Then the Priest, with hands joined, says aloud.
At the Savior's command
and formed by divine teaching,
we dare to say:
The Priest, with hands extended says, and all present continue:
Our Father, who art in heaven,
hallowed be thy name;
thy kingdom come,
thy will be done
on earth as it is in heaven.
Give us this day our daily bread,

and forgive us our trespasses,
as we forgive those who trespass against us;
and lead us not into temptation,
but deliver us from evil.

24   With hands extended, the Priest continues alone:
Deliver us, Lord, we pray, from every evil,
graciously grant peace in our days,
that, by the help of your mercy,
we may be always free from sin
and safe from all distress,
as we await the blessed hope
and the coming of our Savior, Jesus Christ.
He joins his hands. The people conclude the prayer, acclaiming:
For the kingdom, the power and the glory are yours now and for ever.

25   Then the Priest, with hands joined, says quietly:
May the receiving of your Body and Blood,
Lord Jesus Christ,
not bring me to judgment and condemnation,
but through your loving mercy
be for me protection in mind and body
and a healing remedy.

26   The Priest then genuflects, takes a particle,
and holding it slightly raised over the ciborium,
while facing the people, says aloud.
Behold the Lamb of God,
behold him who takes away the sins of the world.
Blessed are those called to the supper of the Lamb.
And together with the people he adds once:
Lord, I am not worthy
that you should enter under my roof,
but only say the word
and my soul shall be healed.

27   And facing the altar, he reverently consumes the Body of Christ,
saying quietly:
May the Body of Christ keep me safe for eternal life.

28   He then proceeds to distribute Communion to the faithful. During
Communion, Psalm 22 (21) or another appropriate chant may be sung.

29   When the distribution of Communion has been completed, the ciborium is taken by the Deacon or another suitable minister to a place pre-

pared outside the church or, if circumstances so require, it is placed in the tabernacle.

30   Then the Priest says:
Let us pray,
and, after a period of sacred silence, if circumstances so suggest, has been observed, he says the Prayer after Communion.
Almighty ever-living God,
who have restored us to life
by the blessed Death and Resurrection of your Christ,
preserve in us the work of your mercy,
that, by partaking of this mystery,
we may have a life unceasingly devoted to you.
Through Christ our Lord.
R. Amen.

31   For the Dismissal the Deacon or, if there is no Deacon, the Priest himself, may say the invitation Bow down for the blessing.

Then the Priest, standing facing the people and extending his hands over them, says this

Prayer over the People:
May abundant blessing, O Lord, we pray,
descend upon your people,
who have honored the Death of your Son
in the hope of their resurrection:
may pardon come,
comfort be given,
holy faith increase,
and everlasting redemption be made secure.
Through Christ our Lord.
R. Amen.

Holy Communion and Worship of the Eucharist Outside Mass
16b   On Good Friday communion may be given only during the celebration of the passion of the Lord; communion may be brought at any hour of the day to the sick who cannot participate in the celebration.

Reflection

The unitive character of the Paschal Triduum and indeed of all time is well exemplified in today's communion rite. Yesterday's service is, as it were, brought forward since all receive the eucharistic bread consecrated during the Holy Thursday liturgy. For its part, the Vigil is recalled in the Prayer after Communion:

God has "restored us to life by the resurrection of Christ." Furthermore, we are propelled even further as "we proclaim the death" of the Lord until he comes.

Suggested Questions for Discussion

1   What possibilities exist as to the musical structure of the communion rite?

2   Should the "Deliver us, Lord . . ." (the embolism) be sung?

3   Why is communion under both kinds not permitted on this day?

Conclusion

Historical Survey

At a time when the liturgies of the Triduum were celebrated in the morning, the Church (especially in monasteries, cathedrals, and other major churches) compensated, as it were, by celebrating in solemn fashion parts of the Divine Office, a celebration having the name *Tenebrae* (Latin meaning darkness or shadows). On Wednesday, Thursday, and Friday evenings of Holy Week a service of matins (an hour of the office with psalms and readings) was celebrated. This was followed by lauds or morning prayer, consisting mostly of psalms and "anticipating" the office of the following day.

A special feature of *Tenebrae* was the use of a large triangular candelabrum (called a hearse). Fifteen lighted candles were placed in the candelabrum; six similar candles were placed on the altar. The candles in the candelabrum were extinguished one after another after each psalm — with one remaining candle in the top place. While the *Benedictus* canticle of lauds was being sung, the six candles on the altar were extinguished so that the last one was extinguished with the canticle's last verse. Finally the one remaining lighted candle was taken behind the altar for a few moments; a noise (*strepitus*) was made, often by all the singers vigorously closing their chant books (for many this was the "high point" of the celebration). The lighted candle, a symbol of the resurrection, was brought back and replaced on the stand. All then departed in silence.

For the most part the service of *Tenebrae* has disappeared with the reform of the liturgy of the hours. The individual "hours" or parts of the liturgy of the hours are to be prayed at their appropriate times of the day. Furthermore, the structure of the hours has now been altered and shortened. And so the traditional *Tenebrae* service has officially ceased to exist. Nonetheless, many of the former texts are still used during the liturgy of the hours as celebrated during the Triduum.

Documentation

Circular Letter "Paschalis sollemnitatis"

71 After the celebration, the altar is stripped; the cross remains however, with four candles. An appropriate place (for example, the chapel of repose used for reservation of the Eucharist on Maundy Thursday) can be prepared within the church, and there the Lord's cross is placed so that the faithful may venerate and kiss it, and spend some time in meditation.

72 Devotions such as the "Way of the Cross," processions of the passion, and commemorations of the sorrows of the Blessed Virgin Mary are not, for pastoral reasons, to be neglected. The texts and songs used, however, should be adapted to the spirit of the Liturgy of this day. Such devotions should be assigned to a time of day that makes it quite clear that the liturgical celebration by its very nature far surpasses them in importance.

Roman Missal

32 And all, after genuflecting to the Cross, depart in silence.

33 After the celebration, the altar is stripped, but the Cross remains on the altar with two or four candlesticks.

34 Vespers (Evening Prayer) is not celebrated by those who have been present at the solemn afternoon liturgical celebration.

Reflection

The letter "*Paschalis sollemnitatis*" recommends that the people's devotion be allowed to express itself outside the church's main celebrations during the Triduum.

Various parishes schedule the traditional stations of the cross, "living" stations of the cross, periods of liturgical music appropriate to the day, etc. Some ethnic communities also have their own forms of Good Friday devotions, for example, processions with a figure of the dead Christ upon a funeral bier. Yet all should be in "the spirit of the liturgy of the day" (*Circular Letter* no. 72).

But now that the whole community gathers in the afternoon or in the early evening for the Good Friday liturgy, the morning hours offer an excellent occasion for celebrating morning prayer, which has long been considered as a sign of the resurrection. As St. Cyprian so wonderfully expressed it: "There should be prayer in the morning so that the resurrection of the Lord may be celebrated" (*On the Lord's Prayer*, 35). Such a celebration, well-planned and faithful to the ritual requirements of all liturgy, offers another opportunity to make holy this most solemn of days.

Suggested Questions for Discussion

1   What should be removed from the sanctuary and when?

2   For how long a period should the cross remain in its place of honor?

3   What can a parish do to promote attendance at morning prayer during the liturgy of the day"?

4   In what way would a popular devotion be in keeping "with the spirit of the day's liturgy"?

HOLY SATURDAY DURING THE DAY

Historical Survey

Primitively, the only observance on Holy Saturday (called the Great Saturday in the Eastern rites) was the continuation of Friday's strict fasting, which was broken by the reception of the Eucharist after midnight during the evening vigil celebration. The day itself focused on Jesus resting in the tomb, his descent among the dead. As Pope Innocent I (d. 417) put it, this was the day when the apostles grieved over the death of Christ.

But as the catechumenate developed, the day was also used for the final preparation of those to be baptized during the Vigil; for example, they recited the creed and received an exorcism.

The anticipation of the Paschal Vigil had a great influence on this day. Once the Vigil was celebrated during the morning hours, a void was created. Lent and especially the Triduum were times for fasting, but now the Triduum was concluded. What to do during Saturday afternoon? Filling in this gap was the blessing of various types of foods; the fast has ended, let us now eat and enjoy!

Documentation

National Statutes for the Catechumenate
15   Candidates for initiation, as well as those who assist them and participate in the celebration of the Easter Vigil with them, are encouraged to keep and extend the paschal fast of Good Friday, as determined by canon 1251, throughout the day of Holy Saturday until the end of the Vigil itself, in accord with the Constitution on the Liturgy, *Sacrosanctum Concilium*, art. 110.

Circular Letter "Paschalis sollemnitatis"
39   The Easter fast is sacred on the first two days of the Triduum, during which, according to ancient tradition, the Church fasts "because the Spouse has been taken away." Good Friday is a day of fasting and abstinence; it is also recommended that Holy Saturday be so observed, in

order that the Church with uplifted and welcoming heart be ready to celebrate the joys of the Sunday of the resurrection.

40   It is recommended that there be a communal celebration of the Office of Readings and Morning Prayer on Good Friday and Holy Saturday. It is fitting that the bishop should celebrate the Office in the cathedral, with as far as possible the participation of the clergy and people.

     This Office, formerly called "Tenebrae," held a special place in the devotion of the faithful as they meditated upon the passion, death and burial of the Lord, while awaiting the announcement of the resurrection.

73   On Holy Saturday the Church is, as it were, at the Lord's tomb, meditating on his passion and death, and on his descent into hell, and awaiting his resurrection with prayer and fasting. It is highly recommended that on this day the Office of Readings and Morning Prayer be celebrated with the participation of the people (cf. n. 40). Where this cannot be done, there should be some celebration of the Word of God, or some act of devotion suited to the mystery celebrated this day.

74   The image of Christ crucified or lying in the tomb, or the descent into hell, which mystery Holy Saturday recalls, as also an image of the sorrowful Virgin Mary can be placed in the church for the veneration of the faithful.

75   On this day the Church abstains strictly from the celebration of the sacrifice of the Mass. Holy Communion may only be given in the form of Viaticum. The celebration of marriages is forbidden, as also the celebration of other sacraments, except those of Penance and the Anointing of the Sick.

76   The faithful are to be instructed on the special character of Holy Saturday. Festive customs and traditions associated with this day on account of the former practice of anticipating the celebration of Easter on Holy Saturday should be reserved for Easter night and the day that follows.

Roman Missal

1   On Holy Saturday the Church waits at the Lord's tomb in prayer and fasting, meditating on his Passion and Death and on his Descent into Hell, and awaiting his Resurrection.

2   The Church abstains from the Sacrifice of the Mass, with the sacred table left bare, until after the solemn Vigil, that is, the anticipation by night of the Resurrection, when the time comes for paschal joys, the abundance of which overflows to occupy fifty days.

3   Holy Communion may only be given on this day as Viaticum.

Rite of Christian Initiation of Adults

Paragraph numbers and citations of the *Rite of Christian Initiation of Adults* subsequently follow the text as approved for use in the dioceses of the United States.

185   In proximate preparation for the celebration of the sacraments of initiation:

1   The elect are to be advised that on Holy Saturday they should refrain from their usual activities, spend their time in prayer and reflection, and, as far as they can, observe a fast.

2   When it is possible to bring the elect together on Holy Saturday for reflection and prayer, some or all of the following rites may be celebrated as an immediate preparation for the sacraments: the presentation of the Lord's prayer, if it has been deferred (see nos. 149, 178–180), the "return" or recitation of the Creed (nos. 193–196), the ephphetha rite (nos. 197–199), the choosing of a baptismal name (nos. 200–202).

186   The choice and arrangement of these rites should be guided by what best suits the particular circumstances of the elect, but the following should be observed with regard to their celebration:

1   In cases where celebration of the presentation of the Creed was not possible, the recitation of the Creed is not celebrated.

2   When both the recitation of the Creed and the ephphetha rite are celebrated, the ephphetha rite immediately precedes the "Prayer before the Recitation" (no. 194).

Reflection

Holy Saturday has been called the Second Sabbath. Like the original Sabbath, it is a day of rest, a day of repose, both physical and spiritual; it is to be a day of fasting and waiting, a day whose quiet is broken only by the morning liturgy of the hours. It should be a time of peace and of prayer whereby, at least in spirit, each member of the community joins those to be baptized in preparing for the events of the coming night. It is a time of preparation, both internal and external.

Suggested Questions for Discussion

1   How can a community promote a spirit of repose on this day, and especially regarding parish liturgy and music directors?

2   What might be appropriate times for the blessing of various foods?

3   What role(s) might the community at large play in today's "retreat" for those preparing for Baptism during the Vigil?

SUNDAY OF THE RESURRECTION (THE EASTER VIGIL IN THE HOLY NIGHT)

Sunday of the Resurrection
(The Easter Vigil in the Holy Night)

SOLEMN BEGINNING OF THE VIGIL OR LUCERNARIUM
Blessing of the Fire
Preparation and Lighting of the Candle
Procession
Easter Proclamation (Exsultet)

LITURGY OF THE WORD
Old Testament Readings / Psalm Responses / Prayers After the Readings
Gloria
Collect
Epistle
Alleluia
Gospel
Homily

BAPTISMAL LITURGY
Presentation of the Candidates
Litany of the Saints
Blessing over the Water
Profession of Faith
Baptism
Explanatory Rites

If No Reception of Candidates into Full Communion	If Reception of Candidates into Full Communion
	Renewal of Baptismal Promises Celebration of Reception
CONFIRMATION	CONFIRMATION Renewal of Promises

LITURGY OF THE EUCHARIST

Dismissal

Introduction

Historical Survey

So central to the liturgical year was the celebration of the Paschal Vigil that St. Gregory of Nazianzus (329–389) spoke of it as the "solemnity of solemnities, far exalted above all others"; Commodian (middle of third century) in Africa called this day the "*dies felicissimus*"; and it was St. Augustine (354–430) in Africa who gave the service its most famous designation, "the mother of all vigils." An inscription (fourth or fifth century) found in a Christian cemetery in central Italy says that a young man died at the "fifth prayer of the night office on Easter night."

A third-century work called the *Teaching of the Apostles* gives us an insight into the content of the observance: "Fast completely on Friday and Saturday, tasting nothing. Gather as one, stay awake, and keep watch throughout the whole night, making supplication, praying, and reading the prophets and the gospel and the psalms with fear and trembling and with diligent supplication until the third hour of the night after Saturday, and then break your fast. . . . Afterwards, offer your sacrifice; then eat, be joyful, rejoice, be happy, because Christ, the pledge of our resurrection, has risen."

The faithful kept vigil "throughout the whole night" since they believed that new life was given to Christ during the night and that the risen Lord would return to this world during the night. Concluding the night watch was the Eucharist, the memorial of the Lord's death and resurrection; by receiving communion one passed from fast to feast, namely, to the beginning of the fifty day feast of Pentecost.

Once the peace of Constantine took effect and Christianity was no longer subject to persecution, the number of converts increased and, accordingly, the structure of the baptismal rites, which came to be celebrated during the vigil, began to expand and develop. Eventually a light ceremony (Jesus being the light that drives away the darkness) opened the celebration. And so it was that by the early thirteenth century all the rites we now associate with the vigil celebration were in place.

Service of Light
Liturgy of Word
Celebration of Baptism
Liturgy of Eucharist

As mentioned earlier, the original Paschal Vigil was a night office, beginning after dark and lasting till well after midnight or even till the break of dawn, but by the seventh century the night vigil had for the most part disappeared. The service eventually began about five in the evening, then at noon, then at eleven in the morning, and finally during the early morning hours, attended by few and with such anomalies as the deacon entering the church with the candle and chanting *"Lumen Christi"* as the rays of the morning sun beamed through stained glass windows into the building. Any semblance of a prolonged night vigil with its symbolism of light conquering darkness had long disappeared.

In 1951, under Pope Pius XII, the Vigil was restored to the evening, and its ceremonies were somewhat altered, both for purposes of the people's participation and for reasons of simplification. This reform led to the rites we celebrate today.

Documentation

General Instruction of the Liturgy of the Hours

211   Night prayer for Holy Saturday is said only by those who are not present at the Easter Vigil.

212   The Easter Vigil takes the place of the office of readings. Those not present at the solemn celebration of the Vigil should therefore read at least four of its readings with the chants and prayers. It is desirable that these be the readings from Exodus, Ezekiel, St. Paul, and from the Gospel. The *Te Deum* follows, then the prayer of the day.

General Norms for the Liturgical Year and the Calendar

18   . . . The solemnity of Easter has the same kind of preeminence in the liturgical year that Sunday has in the week.

21   The Easter Vigil, during the holy night when Christ rose from the dead, ranks as the "mother of all vigils." Keeping watch, the Church awaits Christ's resurrection and celebrates it in the sacraments. Accordingly, the entire celebration of this vigil should take place at night, that is, it should either begin after nightfall or end before the dawn of Sunday.

Instruction "Eucharisticum mysterium"

28   The evening Mass before Easter may not be started before dusk or certainly not before sunset. This Mass is always the Mass of the Easter Vigil, which by reason of its special significance in the liturgical year and in the whole Christian life must be celebrated with the liturgical rites for this holy night according to the rite for the Easter Vigil. . . .

43   It is fitting that small religious communities both clerical and lay, and other lay groups should participate in the celebration of the Easter Triduum in neighboring principal churches.

Similarly where the number of participants and ministers is so small that the celebrations of the Easter Triduum cannot be carried out with the requisite solemnity, such groups of the faithful should assemble in a larger church.

Also where there are small parishes with only one priest, it is recommended that such parishes should assemble, as far as possible, in a principal church and there participate in the celebrations.

According to the needs of the faithful, where a pastor has the responsibility for two or more parishes in which the faithful assemble in large numbers, and where the celebrations can be carried out with the requisite care and solemnity, the celebrations of the Easter Triduum may be repeated in accord with the given norms.

So that seminary students "might live fully Christ's Paschal Mystery, and thus be able to teach those who will be committed to their care," they should be given a thorough and comprehensive liturgical formation. It is important that during their formative years in the seminary they should experience fruitfully the solemn Easter celebrations, especially those over which the bishop presides.

VII. Easter Sunday of the Lord's Resurrection
A. Easter Vigil on the Holiest Night

77   According to a most ancient tradition, this night is "one of vigil for the Lord," and the vigil celebrated during it, to commemorate that holy night when the Lord rose from the dead, is regarded as the "mother of all holy vigils." For in that night the Church keeps vigil, waiting for the resurrection of the Lord, and celebrates the sacraments of Christian initiation.

1 *The Meaning of the Nocturnal Character of the Easter Vigil*

78   "The entire celebration of the Easter Vigil takes place at night. It should not begin before nightfall; it should end before daybreak on Sunday." This rule is to be taken according to its strictest sense. Reprehensible are

those abuses and practices which have crept into many places in violation of this ruling, whereby the Easter Vigil is celebrated at the time of day that it is customary to celebrate anticipated Sunday Masses.

Those reasons which have been advanced in some quarters for the anticipation of the Easter Vigil, such as lack of public order, are not put forward in connection with Christmas night, nor other gatherings of various kinds.

79 The Passover Vigil, in which the Hebrews kept watch for the Lord's Passover which was to free them from slavery to Pharaoh, is an annual commemoration. It prefigured the true Pasch of Christ that was to come, the night that is of true liberation, in which "destroying the bonds of death, Christ rose as victor from the depths."

80 From the very outset the Church has celebrated that annual Pasch, which is the solemnity of solemnities, above all by means of a night vigil. For the resurrection of Christ is the foundation of our faith and hope, and through Baptism and Confirmation we are inserted into the Paschal Mystery of Christ, dying, buried, and raised with him, and with him we shall also reign.

The full meaning of Vigil is a waiting for the coming of the Lord.

2 The Structure of the Easter Vigil and the Significance of its Different Elements and Parts

81 The order for the Easter Vigil is arranged so that after the service of light and the Easter Proclamation (which is the first part of the Vigil), Holy Church meditates on the wonderful works which the Lord God wrought for his people from the earliest times (the second part or Liturgy of the Word), to the moment when, together with those new members reborn in Baptism (third part), she is called to the table prepared by the Lord for his Church — the commemoration of his death and resurrection — until he comes (fourth part).

This liturgical order must not be changed by anyone on his own initiative.

3 Some Pastoral Considerations

93 The Easter Vigil Liturgy should be celebrated in such a way as to offer to the Christian people the riches of the prayers and rites. It is therefore

important that authenticity be respected, that the participation of the faithful be promoted, and that the celebration should not take place without servers, readers and choir exercising their role.

94   It would be desirable if on occasion provision were made for several communities to assemble in one church, wherever their proximity or small numbers mean that a full and festive celebration could not otherwise take place.

The celebration of the Easter Vigil for special groups is not to be encouraged, since above all in this Vigil the faithful should come together as one and should experience a sense of ecclesial community.

The faithful who are absent from their parish on vacation should be urged to participate in the liturgical celebration in the place where they happen to be.

95   In announcements concerning the Easter Vigil care should be taken not to present it as the concluding period of Holy Saturday, but rather it should be stressed that the Easter Vigil is celebrated during Easter night, and that it is one single act of worship. Pastors should be advised that in giving catechesis to the people they should be taught to participate in the Vigil in its entirety.

96   For a better celebration of the Easter Vigil, it is necessary that pastors themselves have an ever deeper knowledge of both texts and rites, so as to give a proper mystagogical catechesis to the people.

Roman Missal

1   By most ancient tradition, this is the night of keeping vigil for the Lord (Ex 12:42), in which, following the Gospel admonition (Lk 12: 35-37), the faithful, carrying lighted lamps in their hands, should be like those looking for the Lord when he returns, so that at his coming he may find them awake and have them sit at his table.

2   Of this night's Vigil, which is the greatest and most noble of all solemnities, there is to be only one celebration in each church. It is arranged, moreover, in such a way that after the Lucernarium and Easter Proclamation (which constitutes the first part of this Vigil), Holy Church meditates on the wonders the Lord God has done for his people from the beginning, trusting in his word and promise (the second part, that is, the Liturgy of the Word) until, as day approaches, with new members

reborn in Baptism (the third part), the Church is called to the table the Lord has prepared for his people, the memorial of his Death and Resurrection until he comes again (the fourth part).

3   The entire celebration of the Easter Vigil must take place during the night, so that it begins after nightfall and ends before daybreak on the Sunday.

4   The Mass of the Vigil, even if it is celebrated before midnight, is a paschal Mass of the Sunday of the Resurrection.

5   Anyone who participates in the Mass of the night may receive Communion again at Mass during the day. A Priest who celebrates or concelebrates the Mass of the night may again celebrate or concelebrate Mass during the day.

The Easter Vigil takes the place of the Office of Readings.

6   The Priest is usually assisted by a Deacon. If, however, there is no Deacon, the duties of his Order, except those indicated below, are assumed by the Priest Celebrant or by a concelebrant.

The Priest and Deacon vest as at Mass, in white vestments.

7   Candles should be prepared for all who participate in the Vigil. The lights of the Church are extinguished.

Reflection

The Paschal Vigil is unique among the celebrations of the Church. It is a time to wait, to watch, to look, to listen, to meditate, to spend time with other Christians and not be restrained by the demands of the hour. The observance is not an anticipated Mass of Easter Sunday. St. Augustine indeed addressed the heart of the matter: "Watch, I tell you, and pray. Let us celebrate this vigil internally and externally. Let God speak to us in these readings. Let us speak to him in our prayers. If we hear his words obediently, he to whom we pray will dwell in us" (Sermon 219). It is about the freedom of prayer.

Suggested Questions for Discussion

1   In what sense may the Paschal Vigil be called the "turning point" of the Triduum?

2   What are the primary symbols of the Easter Vigil?

3   Why is it important that the Vigil start after nightfall and conclude before dawn?

4   How is darkness created?

5   What spaces are needed for celebrating the Vigil?

6   What time constraints, if any, should be considered in planning the Vigil?

7   In communities where there usually are multiple language celebrations, what can be done to accommodate the various language groups and yet have only one Vigil celebration?

8   What can be done so that floral and other decorations do not overwhelm the primary symbols of the celebration?

Bibliography

- "Issues concerning the Celebration of the Easter Vigil. *BCL Newsletter* 32 (January-February 1996).
- "Renewal of Baptismal Promises." *BCL Newsletter* 11 (March 1975).
- "The Easter Vigil and Sunday Obligation." *BCL Newsletter* 12 (February-March 1976).
- "The New *Missale Romanum* and the Easter Vigil." *BCL Newsletter* 39 (December 2001).
- "The Time for the Celebration of the Easter Vigil." *BCL Newsletter* 22 (February 1986).
- "The Time of the Easter Vigil." *BCL Newsletter* 37 (March 2001).
- "The Time of the Easter Vigil." *BCL Newsletter* 37 (December 2001).
- Berger, Ruper and Hans Hollerweger, eds., tr. Matthew J. O'Connell. *Celebrating the Easter Vigil*. New York: Pueblo Publishing Co., 1983.
- Brassard, Ronald E. "Easter Is for Baptism." *Pastoral Music* 6:4 (April-May 1982) 10–11.
- Brassard, Ronald E. "Performed in All Their Fullness and Nobility . . ." *Pastoral Music* 14:3 (February-March 1990), 43–47.
- Buxton, R.F. "Easter." In *The New Westminster Dictionary of Liturgy and Worship*, ed. J.G. Davies. Philadelphia: The Westminster Press, 1986.
- Chupungco, Anscar J. *Shaping the Easter Feast*. Washington, DC, The Pastoral Press, 1992.
- Crichton, J.D., "Paschal Vigil." In *The New Westminster Dictionary of Liturgy and Worship*, ed. J.G. Davies. Philadelphia: The Westminster Press, 1986. 425–426.

- Cunningham, W. Patrick. "Celebrating Easter: A Clue from Gregorian Chant." *Pastoral Music* 9:6 (August-September 1985) 29–32.
- Dopf, Hubert. "Importance and Execution of Song and Music during the Easter Vigil. In *Celebrating the Easter Vigil*, ed. Rupert Berger and Hans Hollerweger. New York: Pueblo Publishing Co., 1983. 119–128.
- Fragomeni, Richard N. "Initiation at Easter: Challenging the Musician." *Pastoral Music* 13:2 (December-January 1989) 31–33.
- Hughes, Kathleen. "Night into Day: The Art of Keeping Vigil." *Assembly* 18:1 (January 1992) 542ff.
- Lengeling, Emil. "Blessing of Baptismal Water in the Roman Rite." *Concilium* 22 (1967) 62–68.
- McNulty, T. Michael. "The 'Secular' Meaning of Easter." *Theology Digest* 22:2 (Summer 1974) 114–116.
- Mitchell, Nathan. "Proclaiming Easter." *Pastoral Music* 19:4 (April-May 1995) 42–46.
- Porter, H. Boone. "Easter and the Mystery of Creation." *Liturgy* 3:1 (Winter 1982) 31–33.
- Regan, Patrick. "The Candle, the Sign of the Crucified." *Liturgy* 3:1 (Winter 1982) 18–21.
- Scheer, A. "Is the Easter Vigil a Rite of Passage?" *Concilium* 112 (1979) 50–61.
- Schwarzenberger, Rudolf. "Easter: The Feast of Feasts." In *Celebrating the Easter Vigil*, ed. Rupert Berger and Hans Hollerweger. New York: Pueblo Publishing Co., 1983. 93–102.
- Stevenson, Kenneth W. "Prayer over Light: A Comparison between the Easter Vigil and Candlemas." *Worship* 64 (January 1990) 2–9.
- Stevenson, Kenneth. "The Ceremonies of Light: Their Shape and Function in the Paschal Vigil Liturgy." *Ephemerides Liturgicae* 99 (March-April 1985) 170–185.
- Vanek, Elisabeth-Anne. "Easter Night: Old Testament Readings." *Assembly* 9:3 (February 1983) 194–195.

Solemn Beginning of the Vigil – Blessing of the Fire

Historical Survey

The origins of the blessing of the new fire, which appeared in Rome's papal liturgy only in the twelfth century, are lost in history. Some historians suggest that this relatively recent addition to the rites of the Paschal Vigil may be traced to a spring pagan festival in which a fire was lighted in honor of the god Wotan (there are some who even credit St. Patrick with "baptizing" this custom). At any rate, the blessing of the fire seems to have migrated to Rome (from Ireland?) by way of northern France and western Germany.

Documentation

Circular Letter "Paschalis sollemnitatis"

82b In so far as possible, a suitable place should be prepared outside the church for the blessing of the new fire, whose flames should be such that they genuinely dispel the darkness and light up the night.

Roman Missal

The Solemn Beginning of the Vigil or Lucernarium
The Blessing of the Fire and Preparation of the Candle

8 A blazing fire is prepared in a suitable place outside the church. When the people are gathered there, the Priest approaches with the ministers, one of whom carries the paschal candle. The processional cross and candles are not carried.

Where, however, a fire cannot be lit outside the church, the rite is carried out as in no. 13, below.

9 The Priest and faithful sign themselves while the Priest says: *In the name of the Father, and of the Son, and of the Holy Spirit*, and then he greets the assembled people in the usual way and briefly instructs them about the night vigil in these or similar words:
Dear brethren (brothers and sisters),
on this most sacred night,
in which our Lord Jesus Christ
passed over from death to life,
the Church calls upon her sons and daughters,
scattered throughout the world,
to come together to watch and pray.
If we keep the memorial
of the Lord's paschal solemnity in this way,
listening to his word and celebrating his mysteries,
then we shall have the sure hope
of sharing his triumph over death
and living with him in God.

10 Then the Priest blesses the fire, saying with hands extended:
Let us pray.
O God, who through your Son
bestowed upon the faithful the fire of your glory,
sanctify ✠ this new fire, we pray,

and grant that,
by these paschal celebrations,
we may be so inflamed with heavenly desires,
that with minds made pure
we may attain festivities of unending splendor.
Through Christ our Lord. R. Amen.

Reflection

In ancient cultures fire was a sign of generation and birth, the guarantee of all good things, a protection against evil influences, the source of both human love and divine power. Yet for the Christian fire is also an image of the wondrous glory of Christ who is the true light of the world, whose death on the cross conquered the darkness of sin and evil.

Suggested Questions for Discussion

1   How large should the Easter fire be?

2   Is it important that all be able to see the fire?

3   Is sound amplification necessary?

4   What provision should be made in case of inclement weather?

5   Might incense be appropriately used during the service of light? If so, when?

Solemn Beginning of the Vigil – Preparation and Lighting of the Candle

Historical Survey

The use of a large, special paschal candle during the Vigil is again a relatively recent addition to the Roman liturgy, first appearing in the papal ceremonies shortly before the twelfth century. Perhaps it was originally connected with the custom of the *lucernarium*, the lighting of the evening candle, a custom observed in both homes and monasteries. At any rate, we find references to such a candle by St. Jerome (c. 342–420) for northern Italy and St. Augustine (354–430) for Africa. In 633 the Fourth Council of Toledo recommended its adoption. In some places the candle was quite tall, for example, at Salisbury Cathedral in England where it was 36 feet in height.

The custom of cutting a cross in the candle with the Greek alpha and omega is already found in a seventh-century liturgical book from Spain. In England Venerable Bede (c. 673–735) speaks about inscribing the year on the candle.

One of the most curious origins of a ceremony in the Roman Rite is that of inserting five grains of incense into the candle. It resulted from a mistranslation. One of the old liturgical books included a prayer requesting that God's blessing come down upon "*hunc incensum [cereum]*," namely, upon "this lighted candle." But later on the phrase was understood as "*hoc incensum*," meaning "this incense." But how much incense? Since the body of Christ had five wounds, it was simply logical to insert five grains of incense into the candle. These various candle rites are now optional.

Documentation

Circular Letter "Paschalis sollemnitatis"

82c   The paschal candle should be prepared, which for effective symbolism must be made of wax, never be artificial, be renewed each year, be only one in number, and be of sufficiently large size so that it may evoke the truth that Christ is the light of the world. It is blessed with the signs and words prescribed in the Missal or by the Conference of Bishops.

Roman Missal

11   After the blessing of the new fire, one of the ministers brings the paschal candle to the Priest, who cuts a cross into the candle with a stylus. Then he makes the Greek letter Alpha above the cross, the letter Omega below, and the four numerals of the current year between the arms of the cross, saying meanwhile:

1.   Christ yesterday and today
     (he cuts a vertical line);
2.   the Beginning and the End
     (he cuts a horizontal line);
3.   the Alpha
     (he cuts the letter Alpha above the vertical line);
4.   and the Omega
     (he cuts the letter Omega below the vertical line).
5.   All time belongs to him
     *(he cuts the first numeral of the current year
     in the upper left corner of the cross);*

6.   and all the ages
     *(he cuts the second numeral of the current year
     in the upper right corner of the cross).*

7.   To him be glory and power
     *(he cuts the third numeral of the current year
     in the lower left corner of the cross);*

8.   through every age and for ever. Amen
     *(he cuts the fourth numeral of the current year
     in the lower right corner of the cross).*

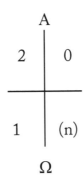

12 When the cutting of the cross and of the other signs has been completed, the Priest may insert five grains of incense into the candle in the form of a cross, meanwhile saying:

(1) By his holy   1
(2) and glorious wounds
(3) may Christ our Lord   4   2   5
(4) guard us
(5) and keep us. Amen.   3

13 Where, because of difficulties that may occur, a fire is not lit, the blessing of fire is adapted to the circumstances. When the people are gathered in the church as on other occasions, the Priest comes to the door of the church, along with the ministers carrying the paschal candle. The people, insofar as is possible, turn to face the Priest.

The greeting and address take place as in no. 9 above; then the fire is blessed and the candle is prepared, as above in nos. 10–12.

14 The Priest lights the paschal candle from the new fire, saying:
May the light of Christ rising in glory
dispel the darkness of our hearts and minds.

As regards the preceding elements, Conferences of Bishops may also establish other forms more adapted to the culture of the different peoples.

Reflection

The paschal candle, always sturdy and robust in size, is a symbol of Christ and the very light that Christ sheds upon all human existence. Maximus of Turin (d. 408/23), a bishop, a poet, and a popular preacher, had this to say: "The light of Christ is not obstructed by walls, nor divided by elements, nor obscured by darkness. Christ's light, I say, is a day without night, a day without end; it is everywhere resplendent, everywhere radiant, everywhere unfailing" (Homily 57).

Then too the candle is a symbol of the pillar of fire and cloud that went before the Israelites as they passed through the Red Sea, from slavery to freedom.

From another perspective and in the words of Pope John Paul II: "In the liturgy of the Easter Vigil the celebrant, as he blesses the candle which symbolizes the risen Christ, proclaims: 'Christ yesterday and today, the beginning and the end, alpha and omega, all time belongs to him, and all the ages, to him be glory and power through every age forever.' He says these words as he inscribes on the candle the numerals of the current year. The meaning of this rite is clear. It emphasizes the fact that Christ is the Lord of time; he is its beginning and its end; every year, every day, and every moment are embraced by his incarnation and resurrection, and thus become part of the 'fullness of time'" (Apostolic Letter *Tertio millennio adveniente* no. 10).

Suggested Questions for Discussion

1   What is to be said of the practice of using the same candle year after year?

2   What should the candle look like?

3   Some parishes decorate the candle with flowers? Good idea or not?

4   What factors would influence a community's decision to use or not to use the optional candle rites?

Solemn Beginning of the Vigil – Procession

Historical Survey

A procession carrying the light into the church seems to have originated in fifth-century Jerusalem, with the practice eventually traveling to Rome by way of Spain and Gaul.

Until the 1951 reform of the paschal vigil this introduction of the light was carried out in a different fashion than we are accustomed to today. A tripartite candle (three candles joined at the foot) or a special brass candlestick was carried in the procession to the paschal candle, which was already located in the sanctuary. It was there that the large candle was lighted from the candle used in the procession. Today's practice is more simple and logical.

It has been suggested that the triple "Light of Christ" originated from a Frankish monastic custom where the light in the refectory (dining hall) was increased by a monk adding more oil to the lamp. Doing so, he chanted "*Lumen Christi*" to which his confreres replied "*Deo gratias.*"

Documentation

Circular Letter "Paschalis sollemnitatis"

83   The procession, by which the people enter the church, should be led by the light of the paschal candle alone. Just as the children of Israel were guided at night by a pillar of fire, so similarly, Christians follow the risen Christ. There is no reason why to each response "Thanks be to God" there should not be added some acclamation in honor of Christ.

The light from the paschal candle should be gradually passed to the candles which it is fitting that all present should hold in their hands, the electric lighting being switched off.

Roman Missal

Procession

15   When the candle has been lit, one of the ministers takes burning coals from the fire and places them in the thurible, and the Priest puts incense into it in the usual way. The Deacon or, if there is no Deacon, another suitable minister, takes the paschal candle and a procession forms. The thurifer with the smoking thurible precedes the Deacon or other min-

ister who carries the paschal candle. After them follows the Priest with the ministers and the people, all holding in their hands unlit candles.

At the door of the church the Deacon, standing and raising up the candle, sings:
The Light of Christ.
Or:
Lumen Christi.
And all reply
Thanks be to God.
Or:
Deo gratias.

The Priest lights his candle from the flame of the paschal candle.

16 Then the Deacon moves forward to the middle of the church and, standing and raising up the candle, sings a second time:
The Light of Christ.
And all reply
Thanks be to God.

All light their candles from the flame of the paschal candle and continue in procession.

17 When the Deacon arrives before the altar, he stands facing the people, raises up the candle and sings a third time:
The Light of Christ.
And all reply
Thanks be to God.

Then the Deacon places the paschal candle on a large candlestand prepared next to the ambo or in the middle of the sanctuary.

And lights are lit throughout the church, except for the altar candles.

Reflection

Just as the Lord led the Israelites during the night by a "column of fire" (Ex 13:21), so Christians are called to follow after Christ who said: "I am the light of the world. Whoever follows me will never walk in darkness but will have the light of life" (Jn 8:12). As baptized Christians we, always in pilgrimage, follow Christ who leads us from the darkness of sin to the light of grace, from death to life, from ignorance to understanding, and from sadness to unending joy. By sharing the light with one another, we show that we too are called to be sources of light for each other.

Suggested Questions for Discussion

1   Which do you prefer? The Latin *Lumen Christi – Deo gratias* or its English translation?

2   What can be done to avoid having the priest or deacon begin the acclamation on too low a pitch?

3   If the church is in darkness, should anything be done to help the people, as they initially enter the building, to see where they are to go?

4   What procedure will be followed for lighting the candles of the people?

5   What type of decorations, if any, will adorn the place where the candle will be placed?

Solemn Beginning of the Vigil – Easter Proclamation (Exsultet)

Historical Survey

Compositions honoring the paschal candle go far back into the history of Christianity. Some believe that initially these were improvised, and only later on were they stabilized and written down. For example, St. Jerome (c. 342–420), when asked to compose such a piece for the deacon Presidius of Piacenza, refused to do so, although he reluctantly agreed to assist in producing such a statement of praise. And from Ennodius (c. 473–521) in Italy we have written examples of two such hymns. Were they sung during the liturgy? We just don't know.

Known as the "Easter Proclamation," the *praeconium paschale* ("paschal praise"), or the *laus cerei* ("praise of the candle"), the text of our present hymn (also called the Exsultet from its first word in Latin) can be traced back to the early eighth century in Gaul. Although it has been suggested that St. Ambrose (c. 339–397) of Milan may have authored the composition, it is more probable that the author, who drew upon the writings of Augustine, Ambrose, and earlier texts, is simply unknown. Another transplant from Gaul, the piece entered the papal liturgy in the eleventh century and wonderfully expresses Christ's redemptive work on our behalf.

The text exists in several traditions and the scribes were not hesitant to make modifications, for example, by omitting the phrase "necessary sin," which some of the clergy believed to be, at the very least, highly offensive. The version we use today has been somewhat abbreviated from that found in the 1570 Missal. Its traditional plainsong melody can be traced back to at least the beginning of the twelfth century.

During the early Middle Ages in Italy the words of the proclamation were written on scrolls with sections of the text interspersed with illuminated pictures. These were inverted in relation to the printing so that the people could view the illustration when the portion of the roll that had been read was allowed to slip down in front of the ambo.

Documentation

Circular Letter "Paschalis sollemnitatis"

84   The deacon makes the Easter Proclamation which tells, by means of a great poetic text, the whole Easter mystery placed in the context of the economy of salvation. In case of necessity, where there is no deacon, and the celebrating priest is unable to sing it, a cantor may do so. The Bishops' Conferences may adapt this proclamation by inserting into it acclamations from the people.

Roman Missal

The Easter Proclamation
(Exsultet)

18   Arriving at the altar, the Priest goes to his chair, gives his candle to a minister, puts incense into the thurible and blesses the incense as at the Gospel at Mass. The Deacon goes to the Priest and saying, Your blessing, Father, asks for and receives a blessing from the Priest, who says in a low voice:
May the Lord be in your heart and on your lips,
that you may proclaim his paschal praise worthily and well,
in the name of the Father and of the Son, ✠ and of the Holy Spirit.
The Deacon replies:
Amen.

This blessing is omitted if the Proclamation is made by someone who is not a Deacon.

19   The Deacon, after incensing the book and the candle, proclaims the Easter Proclamation (Exsultet) at the ambo or at a lectern, with all standing and holding lighted candles in their hands.

The Easter Proclamation may be made, in the absence of a Deacon, by the Priest himself or by another concelebrating Priest. If, however, because of necessity, a lay cantor sings the Proclamation, the words *Therefore, dearest friends* up to the end of the invitation are omitted, along with the greeting *The Lord be with you.*

The Proclamation may also be sung in the shorter form.

Longer Form	**Shorter Form**
Exult, let them exult, the hosts of heaven, exult, let Angel ministers of God exult, let the trumpet of salvation sound aloud our mighty King's triumph! Be glad, let earth be glad, as glory floods her, ablaze with light from her eternal King, let all corners of the earth be glad, knowing an end to gloom and darkness. Rejoice, let Mother Church also rejoice, arrayed with the lightning of his glory, let this holy building shake with joy, filled with the mighty voices of the peoples. [Deacon or Priest only] (Therefore, dearest friends, standing in the awesome glory of this holy light, invoke with me, I ask you, the mercy of God almighty, that he, who has been pleased to number me, though unworthy, among the Levites, may pour into me his light unshadowed, that I may sing this candle's perfect praises).	Exult, let them exult, the hosts of heaven, exult, let Angel ministers of God exult, let the trumpet of salvation sound aloud our mighty King's triumph! Be glad, let earth be glad, as glory floods her, ablaze with light from her eternal King, let all corners of the earth be glad, knowing an end to gloom and darkness. Rejoice, let Mother Church also rejoice, arrayed with the lightning of his glory, let this holy building shake with joy, filled with the mighty voices of the peoples.
(V. The Lord be with you. R. And with your spirit.) V. Lift up your hearts. R. We lift them up to the Lord. V. Let us give thanks to the Lord our God. R. It is right and just.	(V. The Lord be with you. R. And with your spirit.) V. Lift up your hearts. R. We lift them up to the Lord. V. Let us give thanks to the Lord our God. R. It is right and just.
It is truly right and just, with ardent love of mind and heart and with devoted service of our voice, to acclaim our God invisible, the almighty Father, and Jesus Christ, our Lord, his Son, his Only Begotten.	It is truly right and just, with ardent love of mind and heart and with devoted service of our voice, to acclaim our God invisible, the almighty Father, and Jesus Christ, our Lord, his Son, his Only Begotten.

Who for our sake paid Adam's debt
to the eternal Father,
and, pouring out his own dear Blood,
wiped clean the record of our ancient sinfulness.

These, then, are the feasts of Passover,
in which is slain the Lamb, the one true Lamb,
whose Blood anoints the doorposts of believers.

This is the night,
when once you led our forebears,
Israel's children,
from slavery in Egypt
and made them pass dry-shod
through the Red Sea.

This is the night
that with a pillar of fire
banished the darkness of sin.

This is the night
that even now, throughout the world,
sets Christian believers apart from worldly vices
and from the gloom of sin,
leading them to grace
and joining them to his holy ones.

This is the night,
when Christ broke the prison-bars of death
and rose victorious from the underworld.

Our birth would have been no gain,
had we not been redeemed.
O wonder of your humble care for us!
O love, O charity beyond all telling,
to ransom a slave you gave away your Son!

O truly necessary sin of Adam,
destroyed completely by the Death of Christ!

O happy fault
that earned so great, so glorious a Redeemer!

O truly blessed night,
worthy alone to know the time and hour
when Christ rose from the underworld!

This is the night
of which it is written:
The night shall be as bright as day,
dazzling is the night for me,
and full of gladness.

The sanctifying power of this night
dispels wickedness, washes faults away,
restores innocence to the fallen,

Who for our sake paid Adam's debt
to the eternal Father,
and, pouring out his own dear Blood,
wiped clean the record of our ancient sinfulness.

These then are the feasts of Passover,
in which is slain the Lamb, the one true Lamb,
whose Blood anoints the doorposts of believers.

This is the night,
when once you led our forebears,
Israel's children,
from slavery in Egypt
and made them pass dry-shod
through the Red Sea.

This is the night
that with a pillar of fire
banished the darkness of sin.

This is the night
that even now, throughout the world,
sets Christian believers apart from worldly vices
and from the gloom of sin,
leading them to grace
and joining them to his holy ones.

This is the night,
when Christ broke the prison-bars of death
and rose victorious from the underworld.

O wonder of your humble care for us!
O love, O charity beyond all telling,
to ransom a slave you gave away your Son!

O truly necessary sin of Adam,
destroyed completely by the Death of Christ!

O happy fault
that earned so great, so glorious a Redeemer!

The sanctifying power of this night
dispels wickedness, washes faults away,
restores innocence to the fallen,

and joy to mourners, drives out hatred, fosters concord, and brings down the mighty. On this, your night of grace, O holy Father, accept this candle, a solemn offering, the work of bees and of your servants' hands, an evening sacrifice of praise, this gift from your most holy Church. But now we know the praises of this pillar, which glowing fire ignites for God's honor, a fire into many flames divided, yet never dimmed by sharing of its light, for it is fed by melting wax, drawn out by mother bees to build a torch so precious. O truly blessed night, when things of heaven are wed to those of earth, and divine to the human.	and joy to mourners. O truly blessed night, when things of heaven are wed to those of earth and divine to the human. On this, your night of grace, O holy Father, accept this candle, a solemn offering, the work of bees and of your servants' hands, an evening sacrifice of praise, this gift from your most holy Church.
Therefore, O Lord, we pray you that this candle, hallowed to the honor of your name, may persevere undimmed, to overcome the darkness of this night. Receive it as a pleasing fragrance, and let it mingle with the lights of heaven. May this flame be found still burning by the Morning Star: the one Morning Star who never sets, Christ your Son, who, coming back from death's domain, has shed his peaceful light on humanity, and lives and reigns for ever and ever. R. Amen.	Therefore, O Lord, we pray you that this candle, hallowed to the honor of your name, may persevere undimmed, to overcome the darkness of this night. Receive it as a pleasing fragrance, and let it mingle with the lights of heaven. May this flame be found still burning by the Morning Star: the one Morning Star who never sets, Christ your Son, who, coming back from death's domain, has shed his peaceful light on humanity, and lives and reigns for ever and ever. R. Amen.

Reflection

"Sing with the voice, sing with the heart, sing with the mouth. . . . The glory of him who is sung about is nothing other than the one who sings about it. Become yourself the glory that you sing of " (Augustine, Sermon 341).

Suggested Questions for Discussion

1   What principle(s) might govern the choice of the person who will sing the *Exsultet*?

2   Will the long or the short form of the Exsultet be chosen? Why?

3   When should the singing of the Exsultet begin?

4   Is it important that the text be intelligible to the assembly?

5   How long should the electric lighting be left off?

Liturgy of the Word – Old Testament Readings

Historical Survey

The proclamation of the Scriptures, and indeed an abundance of Scripture, lies at the historical heart of the Vigil. The night was long, and the assembly spent its time praying, singing, meditating, and listening. Although initially the lessons may have focused on the death and resurrection of Christ, the gradual development of the baptismal ceremonies during the holy night resulted in readings having baptismal themes, these selections being the last instruction of the catechumens before Baptism.

According to times and places the number of lessons (in the fourteenth and fifteenth centuries they came to be called "prophecies") varied, anywhere from four to ten or more. In some localities each lesson was proclaimed twice, once in Latin and again in Greek.

Today there are seven Old Testament selections, each followed by a psalm and a prayer that is related to the reading.

1   Genesis 1:1–2:2 or Genesis 1:1–26–31a: the creation account, one of the most ancient of the vigil readings.

2   Genesis 22:1–18 or Genesis 22:1–2, 9a, 10–13, 15–18: the story of the sacrifice of Isaac, which has numerous paschal implications; again a traditional reading in the Roman Rite.

3   Exodus 14:15–15:1: the passage through the Red Sea — a figure of Baptism and freedom; a traditional reading, which must always be used.

4   Isaiah 54:5–14: those to be baptized (and people everywhere) are loved by God and are called to enter the new Jerusalem; a recent addition to the list of the vigil readings.

5   Isaiah 55:1–11: the waters of baptism, the bread of life, the word of God — all are invoked in this selection.

6   Baruch 3:9–15, 32–4:4: new life given through water and the Holy Spirit.

7   Ezekiel 36:16–17a, 18–28: "clean water . . . a new heart and . . . a new spirit": the baptismal theme is evident in this new addition; depending on circumstances one may choose among the three texts for the responsorial psalm.

Documentation

Circular Letter "Paschalis sollemnitatis"

85   The readings from Sacred Scripture constitute the second part of the Vigil. They give an account of the outstanding deeds of the history of salvation, which the faithful are helped to meditate calmly upon by the singing of the responsorial psalm, by a silent pause and by the celebrant's prayer.

The restored Order for the Vigil has seven readings from the Old Testament chosen from the Law and the Prophets, which are in use everywhere according to the most ancient tradition of East and West, and two readings from the New Testament, namely from the Apostle and from the Gospel. Thus the Church, "beginning with Moses and all the Prophets" explains Christ's Paschal Mystery. Consequently wherever this is possible, all the readings should be read so that the character of the Easter Vigil, which demands that it be somewhat prolonged, be respected at all costs.

Where, however, pastoral conditions require that the number of readings be reduced, there should be at least three readings from the Old Testament, taken from the Law and the Prophets; the reading from Exodus chapter 14 with its canticle must never be omitted.

86 The typological import of the Old Testament texts is rooted in the New, and is made plain by the prayer pronounced by the celebrating priest after each reading; but it will also be helpful to introduce the people to the meaning of each reading by means of a brief introduction. This introduction may be given by the priest himself or by a deacon.

National or diocesan liturgical commissions will prepare aids for pastors.

Each reading is followed by the singing of a psalm, to which the people respond.

Melodies should be provided for these responses which are capable of promoting the people's participation and devotion. Great care is to be taken that trivial songs do not take the place of the psalms.

Roman Missal

Second Part:
The Liturgy of the Word

20 In this Vigil, the mother of all Vigils, nine readings are provided, namely seven from the Old Testament and two from the New (the Epistle and Gospel), all of which should be read whenever this can be done, so that the character of the Vigil, which demands an extended period of time, may be preserved.

21 Nevertheless, where more serious pastoral circumstances demand it, the number of readings from the Old Testament may be reduced, always bearing in mind that the reading of the Word of God is a fundamental part of this Easter Vigil. At least three readings should be read from the Old Testament, both from the Law and from the Prophets, and their respective Responsorial Psalms should be sung. Never, moreover, should the reading of chapter 14 of Exodus with its canticle be omitted.

22 After setting aside their candles, all sit. Before the readings begin, the Priest instructs the people in these or similar words:
Dear brethren (brothers and sisters),
now that we have begun our solemn Vigil,
let us listen with quiet hearts to the Word of God.
Let us meditate on how God in times past saved his people
and in these, the last days, has sent us his Son as our Redeemer.
Let us pray that our God may complete this paschal work of salvation
by the fullness of redemption.

23   Then the readings follow. A reader goes to the ambo and proclaims the reading. Afterwards a psalmist or a cantor sings or says the Psalm with the people making the response. Then all rise, the Priest says, *Let us pray* and, after all have prayed for a while in silence, he says the prayer corresponding to the reading. In place of the Responsorial Psalm a period of sacred silence may be observed, in which case the pause after *Let us pray* is omitted.

Lectionary for Mass
41   Easter Sunday A B C
                                                    The Resurrection of the Lord
                              At the Easter Vigil in the Holy Night of Easter

Nine readings are assigned to the Easter Vigil: seven from the Old Testament and two from the New. If circumstances demand in individual cases, the number of prescribed readings may be reduced. Three selections from the Old Testament, however, should be read before the epistle and Gospel, although when necessary, two may be read. In any case, the reading from Exodus about the escape through the Red Sea (reading 3) should never be omitted.

First Reading
A Longer Form
>   *God looked at everything he had made, and he found it very good.*
A reading from the Book of Genesis   1:1–2:2

In the beginning, when God created the heavens and the earth,
the earth was a formless wasteland, and darkness covered the abyss,
while a mighty wind swept over the waters.

Then God said,
"Let there be light," and there was light.
God saw how good the light was.
God then separated the light from the darkness.
God called the light "day," and the darkness he called "night."
Thus evening came, and morning followed—the first day.

Then God said,
"Let there be a dome in the middle of the waters,
to separate one body of water from the other."
And so it happened:
God made the dome,
and it separated the water above the dome from the water below it.
God called the dome "the sky."
Evening came, and morning followed—the second day.

Then God said,
"Let the water under the sky be gathered into a single basin,
so that the dry land may appear."
And so it happened:
the water under the sky was gathered into its basin,
and the dry land appeared.
God called the dry land "the earth,"
and the basin of the water he called "the sea."
God saw how good it was.
Then God said,
"Let the earth bring forth vegetation:
every kind of plant that bears seed
and every kind of fruit tree on earth
that bears fruit with its seed in it."
And so it happened:
the earth brought forth every kind of plant that bears seed
and every kind of fruit tree on earth
that bears fruit with its seed in it.
God saw how good it was.
Evening came, and morning followed—the third day.

Then God said:
"Let there be lights in the dome of the sky,
to separate day from night.
Let them mark the fixed times, the days and the years,
and serve as luminaries in the dome of the sky,
to shed light upon the earth."
And so it happened:
God made the two great lights,
the greater one to govern the day,
and the lesser one to govern the night;
and he made the stars.
God set them in the dome of the sky,
to shed light upon the earth,
to govern the day and the night,
and to separate the light from the darkness.
God saw how good it was.
Evening came, and morning followed—the fourth day.

Then God said,
"Let the water teem with an abundance of living creatures,
and on the earth let birds fly beneath the dome of the sky."
And so it happened:
God created the great sea monsters
and all kinds of swimming creatures with which the water teems,
and all kinds of winged birds.
God saw how good it was, and God blessed them, saying,

"Be fertile, multiply, and fill the water of the seas;
and let the birds multiply on the earth."
Evening came, and morning followed—the fifth day.

Then God said,
"Let the earth bring forth all kinds of living creatures:
cattle, creeping things, and wild animals of all kinds."
And so it happened:
God made all kinds of wild animals, all kinds of cattle,
and all kinds of creeping things of the earth.
God saw how good it was.
Then God said:
"Let us make man in our image, after our likeness.
Let them have dominion over the fish of the sea,
the birds of the air, and the cattle,
and over all the wild animals
and all the creatures that crawl on the ground."
God created man in his image;
in the image of God he created him;
male and female he created them.
God blessed them, saying:
"Be fertile and multiply;
fill the earth and subdue it.
Have dominion over the fish of the sea,
the birds of the air,
and all the living things that move on the earth."
God also said:
"See, I give you every seed-bearing plant all over the earth
and every tree that has seed-bearing fruit on it to be your food;
and to all the animals of the land, all the birds of the air,
and all the living creatures that crawl on the ground,
I give all the green plants for food."
And so it happened.
God looked at everything he had made, and he found it very good.
Evening came, and morning followed—the sixth day.

Thus the heavens and the earth and all their array were completed.
Since on the seventh day God was finished
with the work he had been doing,
he rested on the seventh day from all the work he had undertaken.

The word of the Lord.

or

B   Shorter Form
       God looked at everything he had made, and he found it very good.
A reading from the Book of Genesis   1:1, 26–31a

In the beginning, when God created the heavens and the earth,
God said: "Let us make man in our image, after our likeness.
Let them have dominion over the fish of the sea,
the birds of the air, and the cattle, and over all the wild animals
and all the creatures that crawl on the ground.
God created man in his image;
in the image of God he created him;
male and female he created them.
God blessed them, saying:
"Be fertile and multiply;
fill the earth and subdue it.
Have dominion over the fish of the sea, the birds of the air,
and all the living things that move on the earth."
God also said:
"See, I give you every seed-bearing plant all over the earth
and every tree that has seed-bearing fruit on it to be your food;
and to all the animals of the land, all the birds of the air,
and all the living creatures that crawl on the ground,
I give all the green plants for food."
And so it happened.
God looked at everything he had made, and found it very good.

The word of the Lord.

Responsorial Psalm
A   Ps 104:1–2, 5–6, 10, 12, 13–14, 24, 35

R. (30) Lord, send out your Spirit, and renew the face of the earth.

Bless the LORD, O my soul!
O LORD, my God, you are great indeed!
You are clothed with majesty and glory,
robed in light as with a cloak.
R. Lord, send out your Spirit, and renew the face of the earth.

You fixed the earth upon its foundation,
not to be moved forever;
with the ocean, as with a garment, you covered it;
above the mountains the waters stood.
R. Lord, send out your Spirit, and renew the face of the earth.

You send forth springs into the watercourses
that wind among the mountains.
Beside them the birds of heaven dwell;
from among the branches they send forth their song.
R. Lord, send out your Spirit, and renew the face of the earth.

You water the mountains from your palace;
the earth is replete with the fruit of your works.
You raise grass for the cattle,
and vegetation for man's use, producing bread from the earth.
R. Lord, send out your Spirit, and renew the face of the earth.

How manifold are your works, O LORD!
In wisdom you have wrought them all —
the earth is full of your creatures.
Bless the LORD, O my soul!
R. Lord, send out your Spirit, and renew the face of the earth.
or
B   Ps 33:4–5, 6–7, 12–13, 20, and 22
R. (5b) The earth is full of the goodness of the Lord.

Upright is the word of the LORD,
and all his works are trustworthy.
He loves justice and right;
of the kindness of the LORD the earth is full.
R. The earth is full of the goodness of the Lord.

By the word of the LORD the heavens were made;
by the breath of his mouth all their host.
He gathers the waters of the sea as in a flask;
in cellars he confines the deep.
R. The earth is full of the goodness of the Lord.

Blessed the nation whose God is the LORD,
the people he has chosen for his own inheritance.
From heaven the LORD looks down;
he sees all mankind.
R. The earth is full of the goodness of the Lord.

Our soul waits for the LORD,
who is our help and our shield.
May your kindness, O LORD,
be upon us who have put our hope in you.
R. The earth is full of the goodness of the Lord.

Roman Missal
24   After the first reading (about creation: Gen. 1:1–2:2 or 1:1, 26–31a):
        Let us pray.
        Almighty ever-living God,
        who are wonderful in the ordering of all your works,
        may those you have redeemed understand
        that there exists nothing more marvelous
        than the world's creation in the beginning
        except that, at the end of the ages,

Christ our Passover has been sacrificed.
Who lives and reigns for ever and ever.
R. Amen.
Or, On the creation of man:
O God, who wonderfully created human nature
and still more wonderfully redeemed it,
grant us, we pray,
to set our minds against the enticements of sin,
that we may merit to attain eternal joys.
Through Christ our Lord.
R. Amen.

Lectionary for Mass
Second Reading
A   Longer Form

The sacrifice of Abraham our father in faith.

A reading from the Book of Genesis   22:1–18

God put Abraham to the test.
He called to him, "Abraham!"
"Here I am," he replied.
Then God said:
"Take your son Isaac, your only one, whom you love,
and go to the land of Moriah.
There you shall offer him up as a holocaust
on a height that I will point out to you."
Early the next morning Abraham saddled his donkey,
took with him his son Isaac and two of his servants as well,
and with the wood that he had cut for the holocaust,
set out for the place of which God had told him.

On the third day Abraham got sight of the place from afar.
Then he said to his servants:
"Both of you stay here with the donkey,
while the boy and I go on over yonder.
We will worship and then come back to you."
Thereupon Abraham took the wood for the holocaust
and laid it on his son Isaac's shoulders,
while he himself carried the fire and the knife.
As the two walked on together, Isaac spoke to his father Abraham:
"Father!" Isaac said.
"Yes, son," he replied.
Isaac continued, "Here are the fire and the wood,
but where is the sheep for the holocaust?"
"Son," Abraham answered,
"God himself will provide the sheep for the holocaust."
Then the two continued going forward.

When they came to the place of which God had told him,
Abraham built an altar there and arranged the wood on it.
Next he tied up his son Isaac,
and put him on top of the wood on the altar.
Then he reached out and took the knife to slaughter his son.
But the LORD's messenger called to him from heaven,
"Abraham, Abraham!"
"Here I am!" he answered.
"Do not lay your hand on the boy," said the messenger.
"Do not do the least thing to him.
I know now how devoted you are to God,
since you did not withhold from me your own beloved son."
As Abraham looked about,
he spied a ram caught by its horns in the thicket.
So he went and took the ram
and offered it up as a holocaust in place of his son.
Abraham named the site Yahweh-yireh;
hence people now say, "On the mountain the LORD will see."

Again the LORD'S messenger called to Abraham from heaven and said:
"I swear by myself, declares the LORD,
that because you acted as you did
in not withholding from me your beloved son,
I will bless you abundantly
and make your descendants as countless
as the stars of the sky and the sands of the seashore;
your descendants shall take possession
of the gates of their enemies,
and in your descendants all the nations of the earth
shall find blessing—
all this because you obeyed my command."

The word of the Lord.

or

B   Shorter Form
     The sacrifice of Abraham our father in faith.
     A reading from the Book of Genesis   22:1–2, 9a, 10–13, 15–18

God put Abraham to the test.
He called to him, "Abraham!"
"Here I am," he replied.
Then God said:
"Take your son Isaac, your only one, whom you love,
and go to the land of Moriah.
There you shall offer him up as a holocaust
on a height that I will point out to you."

When they came to the place of which God had told him,
Abraham built an altar there and arranged the wood on it.
Then he reached out and took the knife to slaughter his son.
But the LORD's messenger called to him from heaven,
"Abraham, Abraham!"
"Here I am," he answered.
"Do not lay your hand on the boy," said the messenger.
"Do not do the least thing to him.
I know now how devoted you are to God,
since you did not withhold from me your own beloved son."
As Abraham looked about,
he spied a ram caught by its horns in the thicket.
So he went and took the ram
and offered it up as a holocaust in place of his son.

Again the LORD's messenger called to Abraham from heaven and said:
"I swear by myself, declares the LORD,
that because you acted as you did
in not withholding from me your beloved son,
I will bless you abundantly
and make your descendants as countless
as the stars of the sky and the sands of the seashore;
your descendants shall take possession
of the gates of their enemies,
and in your descendants all the nations of the earth
shall find blessing—
all this because you obeyed my command."

The word of the Lord.

Responsial Psalm   16:5, 8, 9–10, 11
R. (1) You are my inheritance, O Lord.

O LORD, my allotted portion and my cup,
you it is who hold fast my lot.
I set the LORD ever before me;
with him at my right hand I shall not be disturbed.
R. You are my inheritance, O Lord.

Therefore my heart is glad and my soul rejoices,
my body, too, abides in confidence;
because you will not abandon my soul to the netherworld,
nor will you suffer your faithful one to undergo corruption.
R. You are my inheritance, O Lord.

You will show me the path to life,
fullness of joys in your presence,

the delights at your right hand forever.
R. You are my inheritance, O Lord.

Roman Missal

25 After the second reading (On Abraham's sacrifice: Gn 22: 1-18 or 1-2, 9a, 10-13, 15-18) and the Psalm (16 [15]).

Let us pray.
O God, supreme Father of the faithful,
who increase the children of your promise
by pouring out the grace of adoption
throughout the whole world
and who through the Paschal Mystery
make your servant Abraham father of nations,
as once you swore,
grant, we pray,
that your peoples may enter worthily
into the grace to which you call them.
Through Christ our Lord.
R. Amen.

Lectionary for Mass

Third Reading

The Israelites marched on dry land through the midst of the sea.
A reading from the Book of Exodus   14:15–15:1

The LORD said to Moses, "Why are you crying out to me?
Tell the Israelites to go forward.
And you, lift up your staff and, with hand outstretched over the sea,
split the sea in two,
that the Israelites may pass through it on dry land.
But I will make the Egyptians so obstinate
that they will go in after them.
Then I will receive glory through Pharaoh and all his army,
his chariots and charioteers.
The Egyptians shall know that I am the LORD,
when I receive glory through Pharaoh
and his chariots and charioteers."

The angel of God, who had been leading Israel's camp,
now moved and went around behind them.
The column of cloud also, leaving the front,
took up its place behind them,
so that it came between the camp of the Egyptians
and that of Israel.
But the cloud now became dark, and thus the night passed
without the rival camps coming any closer together all night long.
Then Moses stretched out his hand over the sea,
and the LORD swept the sea

with a strong east wind throughout the night
and so turned it into dry land.
When the water was thus divided,
the Israelites marched into the midst of the sea on dry land,
with the water like a wall to their right and to their left.

The Egyptians followed in pursuit;
all Pharaoh's horses and chariots and charioteers went after them
right into the midst of the sea.
In the night watch just before dawn
the LORD cast through the column of the fiery cloud
upon the Egyptian force a glance that threw it into a panic;
and he so clogged their chariot wheels
that they could hardly drive.
With that the Egyptians sounded the retreat before Israel,
because the LORD was fighting for them against the Egyptians.

Then the LORD told Moses, "Stretch out your hand over the sea,
that the water may flow back upon the Egyptians,
upon their chariots and their charioteers."
So Moses stretched out his hand over the sea,
and at dawn the sea flowed back to its normal depth.
The Egyptians were fleeing head on toward the sea,
when the LORD hurled them into its midst.
As the water flowed back,
it covered the chariots and the charioteers of Pharaoh's whole army
which had followed the Israelites into the sea.
Not a single one of them escaped.
But the Israelites had marched on dry land through the midst of the sea,
with the water like a wall to their right and to their left.
Thus the LORD saved Israel on that day
from the power of the Egyptians.
When Israel saw the Egyptians lying dead on the seashore
and beheld the great power that the LORD
had shown against the Egyptians,
they feared the LORD and believed in him and in his servant Moses.

Then Moses and the Israelites sang this song to the LORD:
I will sing to the LORD, for he is gloriously triumphant;
horse and chariot he has cast into the sea.

The word of the Lord.

Responsorial Psalm   Ex 15:1–2, 3–4, 5–6, 17–18
R. (1b) Let us sing to the Lord; he has covered himself in glory.

I will sing to the LORD, for he is gloriously triumphant;
horse and chariot he has cast into the sea.

My strength and my courage is the LORD,
and he has been my savior.
He is my God, I praise him;
the God of my father, I extol him.
R. Let us sing to the Lord; he has covered himself in glory.

The LORD is a warrior,
LORD is his name!
Pharaoh's chariots and army he hurled into the sea;
the elite of his officers were submerged in the Red Sea.
R. Let us sing to the Lord; he has covered himself in glory.

The flood waters covered them,
they sank into the depths like a stone.
Your right hand, O LORD, magnificent in power,
your right hand, O LORD, has shattered the enemy.
R. Let us sing to the Lord; he has covered himself in glory.

You brought in the people you redeemed
and planted them on the mountain of your inheritance—
the place where you made your seat, O LORD,
the sanctuary, LORD, which your hands established.
The LORD shall reign forever and ever.
R. Let us sing to the Lord; he has covered himself in glory.

Roman Missal

26   After the third reading (On the passage through the Red Sea: Ex 14: 15-15: 1) and its canticle (Ex 15).

Let us pray.
O God, whose ancient wonders
remain undimmed in splendor even in our day,
for what you once bestowed on a single people,
freeing them from Pharaoh's persecution
by the power of your right hand
now you bring about as the salvation of the nations
through the waters of rebirth,
grant, we pray, that the whole world
may become children of Abraham
and inherit the dignity of Israel's birthright.
Through Christ our Lord.
R. Amen.
Or:
O God, who by the light of the New Testament
have unlocked the meaning
of wonders worked in former times,
so that the Red Sea prefigures the sacred font
and the nation delivered from slavery

foreshadows the Christian people,
grant, we pray, that all nations,
obtaining the privilege of Israel by merit of faith,
may be reborn by partaking of your Spirit.
Through Christ our Lord.
R. Amen.

Lectionary for Mass

Fourth Reading

With enduring love, the Lord your redeemer takes pity on you.
A reading from the Book of the Prophet Isaiah   54:5–14

The One who has become your husband is your Maker;
his name is the LORD of hosts;
your redeemer is the Holy One of Israel,
called God of all the earth.
The LORD calls you back,
like a wife forsaken and grieved in spirit,
a wife married in youth and then cast off, says your God.
For a brief moment I abandoned you,
but with great tenderness I will take you back.
In an outburst of wrath, for a moment
I hid my face from you;
but with enduring love I take pity on you,
says the LORD, your redeemer.
This is for me like the days of Noah,
when I swore that the waters of Noah
should never again deluge the earth;
so I have sworn not to be angry with you,
or to rebuke you.
Though the mountains leave their place
and the hills be shaken,
my love shall never leave you
nor my covenant of peace be shaken,
says the LORD, who has mercy on you.
O afflicted one, storm-battered and unconsoled,
I lay your pavements in carnelians,
and your foundations in sapphires;
I will make your battlements of rubies, your gates of carbuncles,
and all your walls of precious stones.
All your children shall be taught by the LORD,
and great shall be the peace of your children.
In justice shall you be established,
far from the fear of oppression,
where destruction cannot come near you.

The word of the Lord.

Responsorial Psalm   Ps 30:2, 4, 5–6, 11–12, 13
R. (2a) I will praise you, Lord, for you have rescued me.

I will extol you, O LORD, for you drew me clear
and did not let my enemies rejoice over me.
O LORD, you brought me up from the netherworld;
you preserved me from among those going down into the pit.
R I will praise you, Lord, for you have rescued me.

Sing praise to the LORD, you his faithful ones,
and give thanks to his holy name.
For his anger lasts but a moment;
a lifetime, his good will.
At nightfall, weeping enters in,
but with the dawn, rejoicing.
R. I will praise you, Lord, for you have rescued me.

Hear, O LORD, and have pity on me;
O LORD, be my helper.
You changed my mourning into dancing;
O LORD, my God, forever will I give you thanks.
R. I will praise you, Lord, for you have rescued me.

Roman Missal

27   After the fourth reading (On the new Jerusalem: Is 54: 5-14) and the
     Psalm (30 [29]).
     Let us pray.
     Almighty ever-living God,
     surpass, for the honor of your name,
     what you pledged to the Patriarchs by reason of their faith,
     and through sacred adoption increase the children of your promise,
     so that what the Saints of old never doubted would come to pass
     your Church may now see in great part fulfilled.
     Through Christ our Lord.
     R. Amen.

Alternatively, other prayers may be used from among those which
follow the readings that have been omitted.

Lectionary for Mass
Fifth Reading
Come to me that you may have life.
I will renew with you an everlasting covenant.
A reading from the Book of the Prophet Isaiah   55:1–11

Thus says the LORD:
All you who are thirsty,

come to the water!
You who have no money,
come, receive grain and eat;
come, without paying and without cost,
drink wine and milk!
Why spend your money for what is not bread,
your wages for what fails to satisfy?
Heed me, and you shall eat well,
you shall delight in rich fare.
Come to me heedfully,
listen, that you may have life.
I will renew with you the everlasting covenant,
the benefits assured to David.
As I made him a witness to the peoples,
a leader and commander of nations,
so shall you summon a nation you knew not,
and nations that knew you not shall run to you,
because of the LORD, your God,
the Holy One of Israel, who has glorified you.

Seek the LORD while he may be found,
call him while he is near.
Let the scoundrel forsake his way,
and the wicked man his thoughts;
let him turn to the LORD for mercy;
to our God, who is generous in forgiving.
For my thoughts are not your thoughts,
nor are your ways my ways, says the LORD.
As high as the heavens are above the earth,
so high are my ways above your ways
and my thoughts above your thoughts.

For just as from the heavens
the rain and snow come down
and do not return there
till they have watered the earth,
making it fertile and fruitful,
giving seed to the one who sows
and bread to the one who eats,
so shall my word be
that goes forth from my mouth;
my word shall not return to me void,
but shall do my will,
achieving the end for which I sent it.

The word of the Lord.

Responsorial Psalm   Is 12:2–3, 4, 5–6
R. (3) You will draw water joyfully from the springs of salvation.

God indeed is my savior;
I am confident and unafraid.
My strength and my courage is the LORD,
and he has been my savior.
With joy you will draw water
at the fountain of salvation.
R. You will draw water joyfully from the springs of salvation.

Give thanks to the LORD, acclaim his name;
among the nations make known his deeds,
proclaim how exalted is his name.
R. You will draw water joyfully from the springs of salvation.

Sing praise to the LORD for his glorious achievement;
let this be known throughout all the earth.
Shout with exultation, O city of Zion,
for great in your midst
is the Holy One of Israel!
R. You will draw water joyfully from the springs of salvation.

Roman Missal

28   After the fifth reading (On salvation freely offered to all: Is 55: 1-11)
and the canticle (Is 12).

Let us pray.
Almighty ever-living God,
sole hope of the world,
who by the preaching of your Prophets
unveiled the mysteries of this present age,
graciously increase the longing of your people,
for only at the prompting of your grace
do the faithful progress in any kind of virtue.
Through Christ our Lord.
R. Amen.

Lectionary for Mass

Sixth Reading

Walk toward the splendor of the Lord.
A reading from the Book of the Prophet Baruch   3:9–15, 32–4:4

Hear, O Israel, the commandments of life:
listen, and know prudence!
How is it, Israel,
that you are in the land of your foes,
grown old in a foreign land,
defiled with the dead,
accounted with those destined for the netherworld?

You have forsaken the fountain of wisdom!
Had you walked in the way of God,
you would have dwelt in enduring peace.
Learn where prudence is,
where strength, where understanding;
that you may know also
where are length of days, and life,
where light of the eyes, and peace.
Who has found the place of wisdom,
who has entered into her treasuries?

The One who knows all things knows her;
he has probed her by his knowledge—
the One who established the earth for all time,
and filled it with four-footed beasts;
he who dismisses the light, and it departs,
calls it, and it obeys him trembling;
before whom the stars at their posts
shine and rejoice;
when he calls them, they answer, "Here we are!"
shining with joy for their Maker. Such is our God;
no other is to be compared to him:
he has traced out the whole way of understanding,
and has given her to Jacob, his servant,
to Israel, his beloved son.

Since then she has appeared on earth,
and moved among people.
She is the book of the precepts of God,
the law that endures forever;
all who cling to her will live,
but those will die who forsake her.
Turn, O Jacob, and receive her:
walk by her light toward splendor.
Give not your glory to another,
your privileges to an alien race.
Blessed are we, O Israel;
for what pleases God is known to us!

The word of the Lord.

Responsorial Psalm   Ps 19:8, 9, 10, 11
R. (John 6:68c) Lord, you have the words of everlasting life.

The law of the LORD is perfect,
refreshing the soul;
the decree of the LORD is trustworthy,
giving wisdom to the simple.

R. Lord, you have the words of everlasting life.

The precepts of the LORD are right,
rejoicing the heart;
the command of the LORD is clear,
enlightening the eye.
R. Lord, you have the words of everlasting life.

The fear of the LORD is pure,
enduring forever;
the ordinances of the LORD are true,
all of them just.
R. Lord, you have the words of everlasting life.

They are more precious than gold,
than a heap of purest gold;
sweeter also than syrup
or honey from the comb.
R. Lord, you have the words of everlasting life.

Roman Missal

29 After the sixth reading (On the fountain of wisdom: Bar 3: 9-15, 31-4:
4) and the Psalm (19 [18]).
Let us pray.
O God, who constantly increase your Church
by your call to the nations,
graciously grant
to those you wash clean in the waters of Baptism
the assurance of your unfailing protection.
Through Christ our Lord.
R. Amen.

Lectionary for Mass
Seventh Reading
I shall sprinkle clean water upon you and I shall give you a new heart.
A reading from the Book of the Prophet Ezekiel   36:16–17a, 18–28

The word of the LORD came to me, saying:
Son of man, when the house of Israel lived in their land,
they defiled it by their conduct and deeds.
Therefore I poured out my fury upon them
because of the blood that they poured out on the ground,
and because they defiled it with idols.
I scattered them among the nations,
dispersing them over foreign lands;
according to their conduct and deeds I judged them.
But when they came among the nations wherever they came,

they served to profane my holy name,
because it was said of them: "These are the people of the LORD,
yet they had to leave their land."
So I have relented because of my holy name
which the house of Israel profaned
among the nations where they came.
Therefore say to the house of Israel: Thus says the Lord GOD:
Not for your sakes do I act, house of Israel,
but for the sake of my holy name,
which you profaned among the nations to which you came.
I will prove the holiness of my great name, profaned among the nations,
in whose midst you have profaned it.
Thus the nations shall know that I am the LORD, says the Lord GOD,
when in their sight I prove my holiness through you.
For I will take you away from among the nations,
gather you from all the foreign lands,
and bring you back to your own land.
I will sprinkle clean water upon you
to cleanse you from all your impurities,
and from all your idols I will cleanse you.
I will give you a new heart and place a new spirit within you,
taking from your bodies your stony hearts
and giving you natural hearts.
I will put my spirit within you and make you live by my statutes,
careful to observe my decrees.
You shall live in the land I gave your fathers;
you shall be my people, and I will be your God.

The word of the Lord.

Responsorial Psalm
When baptism is celebrated, responsorial psalm A is used;
when baptism is not celebrated, responsorial psalm B or C is used.
A   When baptism is celebrated   Ps 42:3, 5; 43:3, 4

R. (42:2) Like a deer that longs for running streams, my soul longs for you, my God.

Athirst is my soul for God, the living God.
When shall I go and behold the face of God?
R. Like a deer that longs for running streams, my soul longs for you, my God.

I went with the throng
and led them in procession to the house of God,
amid loud cries of joy and thanksgiving,
with the multitude keeping festival.
R. Like a deer that longs for running streams, my soul longs for you, my God.

Send forth your light and your fidelity;
they shall lead me on
and bring me to your holy mountain,
to your dwelling-place.
R. Like a deer that longs for running streams, my soul longs for you, my God.

Then will I go in to the altar of God,
the God of my gladness and joy;
then will I give you thanks upon the harp,
O God, my God!
R. Like a deer that longs for running streams, my soul longs for you, my God.

B   *When baptism is not celebrated*   Is 12:2–3, 4bcd, 5–6

R. (3) You will draw water joyfully from the springs of salvation.

God indeed is my savior;
I am confident and unafraid.
My strength and my courage is the LORD,
and he has been my savior.
With joy you will draw water
at the fountain of salvation.
R. You will draw water joyfully from the springs of salvation.

Give thanks to the LORD, acclaim his name;
among the nations make known his deeds,
proclaim how exalted is his name.
R. You will draw water joyfully from the springs of salvation.

Sing praise to the LORD for his glorious achievement;
let this be known throughout all the earth.
Shout with exultation, O city of Zion,
for great in your midst
is the Holy One of Israel!
R. You will draw water joyfully from the springs of salvation.

C   *When baptism is not celebrated*   Ps 51:12–13, 14–15, 18–19

R. (12a) Create a clean heart in me, O God.

A clean heart create for me, O God,
and a steadfast spirit renew within me.
Cast me not out from your presence,
and your Holy Spirit take not from me.
R. Create a clean heart in me, O God.

Give me back the joy of your salvation,
and a willing spirit sustain in me.

I will teach transgressors your ways,
and sinners shall return to you.
R. Create a clean heart in me, O God.

For you are not pleased with sacrifices;
should I offer a holocaust, you would not accept it.
My sacrifice, O God, is a contrite spirit;
a heart contrite and humbled, O God, you will not spurn.
R. Create a clean heart in me, O God.

Roman Missal

30   After the seventh reading (On a new heart and new spirit: Ez 36: 16-28) and the Psalm (42-43 [41-42]).

Let us pray.
O God of unchanging power and eternal light,
look with favor on the wondrous mystery of the whole Church
and serenely accomplish the work of human salvation,
which you planned from all eternity;
may the whole world know and see
that what was cast down is raised up,
what had become old is made new,
and all things are restored to integrity through Christ,
just as by him they came into being.
Who lives and reigns for ever and ever.
R. Amen.
Or:
O God, who by the pages of both Testaments
instruct and prepare us to celebrate the Paschal Mystery,
grant that we may comprehend your mercy,
so that the gifts we receive from you this night
may confirm our hope of the gifts to come.
Through Christ our Lord.
R. Amen.

Reflection

The Old Testament readings assigned to the Paschal Vigil have been called the very backbone of the night's watch, resounding as they do with numerous melodies singing of the new life won by Christ and shared with us through Baptism. The writers of the New Testament read and knew the writings that formed the basic religious literature of their own time, writings they understood through the filter of their experience of Christ. As a result there is a "mutual illumination" between the Old and the New Testaments. The Christian Testament sheds light upon the Hebrew Scriptures. On the other hand, the Hebrew Scriptures allow us to penetrate the meaning of the New Testament. To state it somewhat differently: "In the Old Testament the New is hidden; in the New Testament the Old appears" (St. Augustine, *Quaest. in Hept 2, 73*). The early Church Fathers, who relied heavily upon the Old Testament in explaining the mysteries of the New Testament and of initiation, were not concerned with abbreviating the Scriptures but with proclaiming them with faith and conviction.

Suggested Questions for Discussion

1   What factors would determine the number of readings to be proclaimed?

2   Is it always advisable to choose the shorter forms of the readings when such are given?

3   It has been said that the Scriptures are to be proclaimed forcefully and with conviction. What does this mean?

4   How can silence be incorporated into the cycle of readings?

5   Do people need to receive special preparation for the Vigil's readings? If so, in what way?

6   May hymns ever replace the psalmody after each reading?

Liturgy of the Word – New Testament Readings

Historical Survey

A unique feature of the Roman Easter Vigil is its separation of the New Testament readings from those of the Old Testament. From early on the Old Testament selections were immediately followed by Baptism or at least the blessing of the baptismal water; perhaps this reflects a time when these lessons served as the immediate preparation of the candidates for Baptism. Then, after the usual prayers that began the Mass (preparatory prayers of the priest which were added only during the Middle Ages, the *Gloria*, the collect) there followed the first New Testament reading, Colossians 3:1–4 ("If then you were raised with Christ, seek what is above . . ."). Then a triple Alleluia was sung, followed by a short verse and the psalm *Laudate*, all of which led to the gospel, Matthew 28:5–6.

Today, however, the sequence is different and somewhat more logical. After the Old Testament readings the *Gloria* is sung, followed by the opening prayer, the first reading (Rom 6:3–11), the Alleluia and the responsorial psalm, and the Gospel, which differs each year according to the A, B, C cycles. It is only after the Gospel that the liturgy of initiation is celebrated.

As to the use of the *Gloria*, this hymn has always had a close connection to Easter since it originated in the East as a resurrection hymn to be sung at dawn. When it entered the western liturgy, the piece could only be used at celebrations presided over by the pope or bishop; an exception, however, was made for priests when they presided at the Easter Vigil. The custom of ringing the church bells during the singing of the hymn is first noted in tenth-century England and seemingly had become widespread on the continent by the late thirteenth century.

Our present rubrics suggest that, all things being equal, the priest himself is to intone the triple Alleluia. This custom dates back to early times and appears to be attested by St. Jerome (c. 342–420) who wrote that the bishop's proclamation of the Resurrection at the altar is of "remote antiquity."

Documentation

Circular Letter "Paschalis sollemnitatis"

87   After the readings from the Old Testament, the hymn *"Gloria in excelsis"* is sung, the bells are rung in accordance with local custom, the collect is recited, and the celebration moves on to the readings from the New Testament. An exhortation from the Apostle on Baptism as an insertion into Christ's Paschal Mystery is read.

Then all stand and the priest intones the "Alleluia" three times, each time raising the pitch. The people repeat it after him. If it is necessary, the psalmist or cantor may sing the "Alleluia," which the people then take up as an acclamation to be interspersed between the verses of Psalm 117, so often cited by the Apostles in their Easter preaching. Finally, the resurrection of the Lord is proclaimed from the Gospel as the high point of the whole Liturgy of the Word. After the Gospel a homily is to be given, no matter how brief.

Roman Missal

31   After the last reading from the Old Testament with its Responsorial Psalm and its prayer, the altar candles are lit, and the Priest intones the

hymn *Gloria in excelsis Deo* (Glory to God in the highest), which is taken up by all, while bells are rung, according to local custom.

32   When the hymn is concluded, the Priest says the Collect in the usual way.

Let us pray.
O God, who make this most sacred night radiant
with the glory of the Lord's Resurrection,
stir up in your Church a spirit of adoption,
so that, renewed in body and mind,
we may render you undivided service.
Through our Lord Jesus Christ, your Son,
who lives and reigns with you in the unity of the Holy Spirit,
one God, for ever and ever.

33   Then the reader proclaims the reading from the Apostle.

Lectionary for Mass

Epistle

Christ, raised from the dead, dies no more.
A reading from the Letter of Saint Paul to the Romans   6:3–11

Brothers and sisters:
Are you unaware that we who were baptized into Christ Jesus
were baptized into his death?
We were indeed buried with him through baptism into death,
so that, just as Christ was raised from the dead
by the glory of the Father,
we too might live in newness of life.

For if we have grown into union with him through a death like his,
we shall also be united with him in the resurrection.
We know that our old self was crucified with him,
so that our sinful body might be done away with,
that we might no longer be in slavery to sin.
For a dead person has been absolved from sin.
If, then, we have died with Christ,
we believe that we shall also live with him.
We know that Christ, raised from the dead, dies no more;
death no longer has power over him.
As to his death, he died to sin once and for all;
as to his life, he lives for God.
Consequently, you too must think of yourselves as being dead to sin
and living for God in Christ Jesus.

The word of the Lord.

Roman Missal

Alleluia

34   After the Epistle has been read, all rise, then the Priest solemnly intones the Alleluia three times, raising his voice by a step each time, with all repeating it. If necessary, the psalmist intones the Alleluia.

Then the psalmist or cantor proclaims Psalm 118 (117) with the people responding Alleluia.

Lectionary for Mass

Responsorial Psalm   Ps 118:1–2, 16–17, 22–23
R. Alleluia, alleluia, alleluia.

Give thanks to the LORD, for he is good,
for his mercy endures forever.
Let the house of Israel say,
"His mercy endures forever."
R. Alleluia, alleluia, alleluia.

The right hand of the LORD has struck with power;
the right hand of the LORD is exalted.
I shall not die, but live,
and declare the works of the LORD.
R. Alleluia, alleluia, alleluia.

The stone the builders rejected
has become the cornerstone.
By the LORD has this been done;
it is wonderful in our eyes.
R. Alleluia, alleluia, alleluia.

Roman Missal

Gospel

35   The Priest, in the usual way, puts incense in the thurible and blesses the Deacon. At the Gospel lights are not carried, but only incense.

Lectionary for Mass

Gospel
A
        He has been raised from the dead
            and is going before you to Galilee.
A reading from the holy Gospel according to Matthew   28:1–10

After the sabbath, as the first day of the week was dawning,
Mary Magdalene and the other Mary came to see the tomb.
And behold, there was a great earthquake;

for an angel of the Lord descended from heaven,
approached, rolled back the stone, and sat upon it.
His appearance was like lightning
and his clothing was white as snow.
The guards were shaken with fear of him
and became like dead men.
Then the angel said to the women in reply,
"Do not be afraid!
I know that you are seeking Jesus the crucified.
He is not here, for he has been raised just as he said.
Come and see the place where he lay.
Then go quickly and tell his disciples,
'He has been raised from the dead,
and he is going before you to Galilee;
there you will see him.'
Behold, I have told you."
Then they went away quickly from the tomb,
earful yet overjoyed,
and ran to announce this to his disciples.
And behold, Jesus met them on their way and greeted them.
They approached, embraced his feet, and did him homage.
Then Jesus said to them, "Do not be afraid.
Go tell my brothers to go to Galilee,
and there they will see me."

The Gospel of the Lord.

B

Jesus of Nazareth, the crucified, has been raised.
A reading from the holy Gospel according to Mark   16:1–7
When the sabbath was over,
Mary Magdalene, Mary, the mother of James, and Salome
bought spices so that they might go and anoint him.
Very early when the sun had risen,
on the first day of the week, they came to the tomb.
They were saying to one another,
"Who will roll back the stone for us
from the entrance to the tomb?"
When they looked up,
they saw that the stone had been rolled back;
it was very large.
On entering the tomb they saw a young man
sitting on the right side, clothed in a white robe,
and they were utterly amazed.
He said to them, "Do not be amazed!
You seek Jesus of Nazareth, the crucified.
He has been raised; he is not here.
Behold the place where they laid him.

But go and tell his disciples and Peter,
'He is going before you to Galilee;
there you will see him, as he told you.'"

The Gospel of the Lord.

C

Why do you seek the Living One among the dead?
A reading from the holy Gospel according to Luke   24:1–12
At daybreak on the first day of the week
the women who had come from Galilee with Jesus
took the spices they had prepared
and went to the tomb.
They found the stone rolled away from the tomb;
but when they entered,
they did not find the body of the Lord Jesus.
While they were puzzling over this, behold,
two men in dazzling garments appeared to them.
They were terrified and bowed their faces to the ground.
They said to them,
"Why do you seek the living one among the dead?
He is not here, but he has been raised.
Remember what he said to you while he was still in Galilee,
that the Son of Man must be handed over to sinners
and be crucified, and rise on the third day."
And they remembered his words.
Then they returned from the tomb
and announced all these things to the eleven
and to all the others.
The women were Mary Magdalene, Joanna,
and Mary the mother of James;
the others who accompanied them also told this
to the apostles, but their story seemed like nonsense
and they did not believe them.
But Peter got up and ran to the tomb,
bent down, and saw the burial cloths alone;
then he went home amazed at what had happened.

The Gospel of the Lord.

Roman Missal

Homily

36   After the Gospel, the Homily, even if brief, is not to be omitted.

Rite of Christian Initiation of Adults

566b The homily should include references not only to the sacraments of initiation but also to reception and full communion (see no. 489).

Reflection

It is especially at this point in the Vigil celebration that we begin to experience grateful joy, profound happiness. The singing of the *Gloria*, the readings and psalm, all tell us that this indeed "is the day the Lord has made." We have reached the end of a journey, one consisting of prayer, fasting, and almsgiving. Now is the time when, through the grace of God, we will bear the good fruit of what has been planted.

Musically, it is the singing of the Alleluia that so well reflects our belief in what Christ has gained for us, in what we are now celebrating. As St. Augustine (354–430) phrased it: "These are the days when we hear 'Alleluia' and our spirit is somehow transformed. Do we not get a certain foretaste of that city on high? Behold we chant 'Alleluia'. It is good, it is joyful, it is full of joy, grace, and tenderness."

Suggested Questions for Discussion

1   What is the musical highlight of the liturgy of the word? The Gloria or the Alleluia?

2   In what non-musical ways may the singing of the Gloria and the Alleluia be highlighted?

3   Why, all things being equal, is the presider to intone the Alleluia?

4   Why are candles not used in the gospel procession?

5   How elaborate a homily is needed during this celebration? What might be its theme(s)?

Celebration of Baptism – Introduction

Historical Survey

The early Church was strongly influenced by St. Paul's explanation of the link between Baptism and Christ's passage from death to life: "Do you not know that all of us who have been baptized into Christ Jesus were baptized into his death"

(Rom 6:3)? And so by the early third century baptisms were celebrated during the Paschal Vigil (as well as at the conclusion of Easter's fifty day extension, namely, the Pentecost Vigil). "Easter stands out as the more solemn day for baptism since the Lord's Passion in which we are baptized is therein completed. . . . Next, the time of Pentecost is a most propitious time for celebrating baptism," wrote Tertullian (c. 160–c. 200) in his treatise *On Baptism* 19, 2.

After the days of persecution ended, many men, women, and children sought admission into the Christian community, which was now in a position to develop its liturgical, catechetical, and other structures, both those preparatory to Baptism and those taking place on the days immediately thereafter. It is from such instruction that we have the baptismal catechesis of such famous bishops as Ambrose of Milan (c. 339–397), Cyril of Jerusalem (c. 315–386) or his successor John of Jerusalem, Theodore of Mopsuestia (c. 350–428), John Chrysostom (c. 347–407) and others.

For centuries Christian initiation took place primarily during the Easter Vigil, and in many areas its structure was: 1. the water bath; 2. the anointing by the bishop or what we now call Confirmation; 3. the reception of the Eucharist.

But from the sixth century onward, the Paschal Vigil as a time for initiation was gradually being abandoned, at least outside Rome. More and more the candidates for "illumination," as Baptism was called (see Eph 5:14), were no longer adults but children. Since this was a period of high infant mortality, effort was placed on baptizing them as soon as possible (*quam primum*) in order to free these infants from original sin, a doctrine whose classical formulation was elaborated by St. Augustine (354–430). The practice of baptizing soon after birth separated the water bath from the post-baptismal anointing always conferred by the bishop, and greatly influenced the future history of Confirmation. Nonetheless, Rome up to the twelfth century held fast to the traditional practice of baptizing only during the Vigil. Eventually the rubric for Holy Saturday in the Missal read: "If there are any candidates for baptism he [the priest] baptizes them in the usual manner."

It was only with the publication of the Rite of Christian Initiation of Adults in 1972 and the Rite of Baptism for Children in 1973 that emphasis was placed on celebrating baptisms, both of adults and children, during the Paschal Vigil.

Documentation

Circular Letter "Paschalis sollemnitatis"

88a   The third part of the Vigil is the baptismal liturgy. Christ's Passover and ours is now celebrated. This is given full expression in those churches which have a baptismal font, and more so when the Christian initiation of adults is held, or at least the Baptism of infants.

Rite of Christian Initiation of Adults

8   The whole initiation must bear a markedly paschal character, since the initiation of Christians is the first sacramental sharing in Christ's dying and rising and since, in addition, the period of purification and enlightenment ordinarily coincides with Lent and the period of postbaptismal catechesis or mystagogy with the Easter season. All the resources of Lent should be brought to bear as a more intense preparation of the elect and the Easter Vigil should be regarded as the proper time for the sacraments of initiation. Because of pastoral needs, however, the sacraments of initiation may be celebrated at other times (see nos. 26–30).

206   The third step in the Christian initiation of adults is the celebration of the sacraments of baptism, confirmation, and Eucharist. Through this final step the elect, receiving pardon for their sins, are admitted into the people of God. They are graced with adoption as children of God and are led by the Holy Spirit into the promised fullness of time begun in Christ and, as they share in the eucharistic sacrifice and meal, even to a foretaste of the kingdom of God.

207   The usual time for the celebration of the sacraments of initiation is the Easter Vigil (see no. 23), at which preferably the bishop himself presides as celebrant, at least for the initiation of those who are fourteen years old or older [. . .]

Rite of Baptism for Children, Introduction, 2nd editio typica

28   When the baptism of children is celebrated as part of the Easter Vigil, the ritual should be arranged as follows:

1   At a convenient time and place before the Easter Vigil the rite of receiving the children is celebrated. The liturgy of the word may be omitted at the end, according to the circumstances, and the prayer of exorcism is said, followed by the anointing with the oil of catechumens.

2   The celebration of the sacrament (nos. 56–58, 60–63) takes place after the blessing of the water, as is indicated in the rite of the Easter Vigil.

3   The assent of the celebrant and community (no. 59) is omitted, as are the presentation of the lighted candle (no 64) and the ephphetha rite (no. 65)

4   The conclusion of the rite (nos. 67–71) is omitted.

National Statutes for the Catechumenate

14   In order to signify clearly the interrelation or coalescence of the three sacraments which are required for full Christian initiation (canon 842:2), adult candidates, including children of catechetical age, are to receive baptism, confirmation, and eucharist in a single eucharistic celebration, whether at the Easter Vigil or, if necessary, at some other time.

18   Since children who have reached the use of reason are considered, for purposes of Christian initiation, to be adults (canon 852:1) . . . they should receive the sacraments of baptism, confirmation, and eucharist at the Easter Vigil, together with older catechumens.

Reflection

"O Night brighter than day;
O Night brighter than the sun;
O Night whiter than snow;
O Night more brilliant than torches;
O Night more delightful than paradise;
O Night which knows not darkness;
O Night which has banished sleep;
O Night which has taught us to join vigil with angels;
O Night terror of demons;
O Night most desirable in the year;
O Night of torchbearing of the bridegroom in the Church;
O Night mother of the newly baptized;
O Night when the devil slept and was stripped;
O Night in which the Inheritor brought the beneficiaries
   into their inheritance;
An inheritance without end."
(Asterius of Amasea [d. 410])

Suggested Questions for Discussion

1   What effect does the decision not to celebrate Baptism during the Vigil have on the Vigil's celebration?

2   How are the catechumens "incorporated" into the community even before their ritual initiation?

3   How important is what has been called the principle of "liberality" during the celebration of Baptism, and indeed throughout the Triduum?

4   What changes need to be made to the celebration when infants — in addition to adults — are baptized during the Vigil?

Celebration of Baptism – Presentation of Candidates and Prayer

Historical Survey

Some type of formal attestation on behalf of the adults to be baptized has long been a traditional practice in Christian initiation, at least in certain geographical areas. In the third-century, according to the Apostolic Tradition once ascribed to Hippolytus, this giving of witness occurred early during the catechumenate: "Let [the candidates] be examined as to the reason why they have come forward to the faith. And those who bring them shall bear witness for them. . . . Let their life and manner of life be inquired into." And as the day for Baptism approached, their lives were "to be examined, whether they lived piously."

But once the majority of those being baptized were infants and no longer adults, the catechumenate as a living ongoing ecclesial reality was reduced to its liturgical elements alone; focus came to be placed on the parents and godparents. For example, in the rites before Baptism the priest inquired as to the worthiness of the parents presenting the baby for Baptism. And in the 1517 Ritual he began the ceremony of baptizing infants by inquiring: "What do you ask of God's Church?" And the sponsor replied: "Faith." In the 1969 revision of the rite for infant Baptism the response — now by the parents — is "Baptism." As to adult candidates for Baptism, it is their godparents who, in the name of the Church, attest to their worthiness.

Documentation

Third Part:
Baptismal Liturgy

37   After the Homily the Baptismal Liturgy begins. The Priest goes with the ministers to the baptismal font, if this can be seen by the faithful. Otherwise a vessel with water is placed in the sanctuary.

38   Catechumens, if there are any, are called forward and presented by their godparents in front of the assembled Church or, if they are small children, are carried by their parents and godparents.

39   Then, if there is to be a procession to the baptistery or to the font, it forms immediately. A minister with the paschal candle leads off, and those to be baptized follow him with their godparents, then the ministers, the Deacon, and the Priest. During the procession, the Litany (n. 43) is sung. When the Litany is completed, the Priest gives the address (n. 40).

Reflection

Before all else, Baptism is the "sacrament of faith," a sacrament celebrated within a community of faith, amidst a believing people. There simply can be no sacrament of Baptism without faith.

To celebrate the sacraments of initiation requires that a choice has been made, either on the part of the adults or older children who are presenting themselves for Baptism or on the part of the parents who ask that their infants be baptized. To be sure, God's grace is always present, and the Church is always eager to extend a welcome to new members. Yet more is required. For adults and older children, not only is doctrinal instruction required but also participation in the Church's life of prayer and good works — as attested by each candidate's godparent at the Rite of Election and now, once again, immediately before Baptism itself. As to infants, it is the parents, assisted by the godparents, who are responsible for the further nurturing and growth of God's baptismal grace given at Baptism. Their role at the sacramental celebration is not one of being "stand-ins"; rather, they act and speak in their own names.

Suggested Questions for Discussion

1   Is it a good idea for the catechumens and other candidates to "rehearse" the baptismal ceremonies which take place during the Vigil?

2   If not, what type of ritual preparation should they receive?

3   Might the presentation of the catechumens and other candidates be made part of the homily?

4   What factors would determine whether baptisms should be celebrated in the sanctuary or in the baptistery?

5   Are all the members of the assembly able to see what will occur during the baptism?

Celebration of Baptism – Litany of the Saints

Historical Survey

A litany (from the Greek *lité* meaning supplication or petition) is one of the most ancient forms of Christian prayer; it consists of a series of requests, said or sung, to which there is a fixed response. This type of prayer can be traced back to fourth-century Antioch from which it soon spread to Constantinople and then to Rome. Among its forms in the Roman liturgy are the general intercessions and the Lamb of God; in the East the litany is a major liturgical element, especially in liturgies of the Byzantine family.

As to the litany of the saints, this prayer has come down to us in various versions. That used on Holy Saturday is a shortened form; traditionally each petition and response were doubled, and in some areas they were repeated up to seven times. First appearing in the Roman papal liturgy as early as 650–700, this litany has historically been "processional music" occurring at various locations in the baptismal rite: the whole litany being sung either as the ministers and candidates moved to the font or as they returned from the font; or the first half of the litany being sung on the way to the baptistery and the second half sung when the ministers return.

Today the litany retains its function as processional music only when Option B for the presentation of the candidates is chosen. In Options A and C it is sung only after the ministers, candidates, and godparents have assembled at the font.

Documentation

Roman Missal

40   If, however, the Baptismal Liturgy takes place in the sanctuary, the Priest immediately makes an introductory statement in these or similar words.

If there are candidates to be baptized:
Dearly beloved,
with one heart and one soul, let us by our prayers
come to the aid of these our brothers and sisters in their blessed hope,
so that, as they approach the font of rebirth,
the almighty Father may bestow on them
all his merciful help.
If the font is to be blessed, but no one is to be baptized:
Dearly beloved,
let us humbly invoke upon this font
the grace of God the almighty Father,
that those who from it are born anew
may be numbered among the children of adoption in Christ.

41   The Litany is sung by two cantors, with all standing (because it is Easter Time) and responding.

If, however, there is to be a procession of some length to the baptistery, the Litany is sung during the procession; in this case, those to be baptized are called forward before the procession begins, and the procession takes place led by the paschal candle, followed by the catechumens with their godparents, then the ministers, the Deacon, and the Priest. The address should occur before the Blessing of Water.

42   If no one is to be baptized and the font is not to be blessed, the Litany is omitted, and the Blessing of Water (no. 54) takes place at once.

43   In the Litany the names of some Saints may be added, especially the Titular Saint of the church and the Patron Saints of the place and of those to be baptized.

If there are candidates to be baptized, the Priest, with hands extended, says the following prayer:

Almighty ever-living God,
be present by the mysteries of your great love
and send forth the spirit of adoption
to create the new peoples
brought to birth for you in the font of Baptism,
so that what is to be carried out by our humble service
may be brought to fulfillment by your mighty power.
Through Christ our Lord.
R. Amen.

Reflection

Devotion to the saints, namely, those men and women who have lived out their baptismal commitment in a special way, extends far back into the history of Christianity. Already early on, it was but a short step from honoring such persons in a particular way to acknowledging the intercessory power of these elders in the faith.

A person is baptized into a Church which in turn is part of a communion of saints that extends beyond this earth. All Christians, both those inhabiting this world as well as those who have passed on to the fullness of God's kingdom, have a stake in every Baptism. As St. Augustine (354–430) wrote: "A Christian people celebrates together in religious solemnity the memorials of the martyrs . . . so that it can . . . be aided by their prayers" (*Against Faustus the Manichean* 20, 21).

Suggested Questions for Discussion

1   What would determine whether the litany is sung or recited?

2   Who should lead the litany?

3   What should be its pace?

4   How may the litany be adapted to the place, the catechumens, and the other candidates?

Celebration of Baptism –
Blessing of Water

Historical Survey

The custom of blessing the water to be used for Baptism, a rite that can be traced back to the beginning of the third century, perhaps began once the water bath no longer took place outdoors on the banks of rivers and streams.

The text, quite lengthy, used for centuries in the Roman rite for this blessing was a mixture of Roman and other elements, and perhaps already existed, at least in part, during the fifth and sixth centuries. Its style has led some to compare it to the eucharistic prayer proclaimed during Mass. The bishop and eventually the priest invoked both Old and New Testament images of water that not only purifies but also gives new life. Eventually a number of actions were added to give dramatic impact to the text, for example, a triple breathing upon the water took place in conjunction with an invocation of the Holy Spirit (who came down upon the waters at creation); a touching or signing the water with the hand; the infusion of oil and chrism (apparently this was a Gallican practice) into the water (to perfume the oil — seen as a symbol of the Holy Spirit); and finally the lowering of two candles and eventually only the paschal candle into the water — the meaning here was that the Holy Spirit descends like light or that Christ the light (or Christ who died and rose) descends upon the water, and yet there was a certain sexual meaning here since the water of Baptism was considered the womb of the Church. The presider said: "May the power of the Holy Spirit descend into all the water of this font."

One result of the post-Vatican II liturgical reform has been that this blessing prayer has been revised, and to such an extent that almost an entirely new text, much shorter than the old, has been created. Nonetheless, the strong biblical images of cleansing and new birth have been retained. Chrism is no longer poured into the water. In fact, the number of gestures has been reduced to one: either touching the water or lowering the Easter candle into it.

So important is this prayer to the Vigil that the water may be blessed even if there are no baptismal candidates present, as long as the church is one in which baptisms are ordinarily celebrated.

Documentation

Circular Letter "Paschalis sollemnitatis"

88b   Even if there are no candidates for Baptism, the blessing of baptismal water should still take place in parish churches. If this blessing does not take place at the baptismal font, but in the sanctuary, baptismal water should be carried afterwards to the baptistry there to be kept throughout the whole of paschal time. Where there are neither candidates for Baptism nor any need to bless the font, Baptism should be commemorated by the blessing of water destined for sprinkling upon the people.

Rite of Christian Initiation of Adults

21   The water blessed at the Easter Vigil should, if possible, be kept and used throughout the Easter season to signify more clearly the relationship between the sacrament of baptism and the paschal mystery. Outside the Easter season, it is desirable that the water be blessed for each occasion, in order to express clearly through the words of blessing the mystery of salvation that the Church recalls and proclaims. If the baptistery is supplied with running water, the blessing is given to the water as it flows.

210   PRAYER OVER THE WATER: The celebration of baptism begins with the blessing of water [. . .] The blessing declares the religious meaning of water as God's creation and the sacramental use of water in the unfolding of the paschal mystery, and the blessing is also a remembrance of God's wonderful works in the history of salvation.

The blessing thus introduces an invocation of the Trinity at the very outset of the celebration of baptism. For it calls to mind the mystery of God's love from the beginning of the world and the creation of the human race; by invoking the Holy Spirit and proclaiming Christ's death and resurrection, it impresses on the mind the newness of Christian baptism, by which we share in his own death and resurrection and receive the holiness of God himself.

Roman Missal

Blessing of Baptismal Water

46   The Priest then blesses the baptismal water, saying the following prayer with hands extended:
O God, who by invisible power
accomplish a wondrous effect

through sacramental signs
and who in many ways have prepared water, your creation,
to show forth the grace of Baptism;
O God, whose Spirit
in the first moments of the world's creation
hovered over the waters,
so that the very substance of water
would even then take to itself the power to sanctify;
O God, who by the outpouring of the flood
foreshadowed regeneration,
so that from the mystery of one and the same element of water
would come an end to vice and a beginning of virtue;
O God, who caused the children of Abraham
to pass dry-shod through the Red Sea,
so that the chosen people,
set free from slavery to Pharaoh,
would prefigure the people of the baptized;
O God, whose Son,
baptized by John in the waters of the Jordan,
was anointed with the Holy Spirit,
and, as he hung upon the Cross,
gave forth water from his side along with blood,
and after his Resurrection, commanded his disciples:
"Go forth, teach all nations, baptizing them
in the name of the Father and of the Son and of the Holy Spirit,"
look now, we pray, upon the face of your Church
and graciously unseal for her the fountain of Baptism.
May this water receive by the Holy Spirit
the grace of your Only Begotten Son,
so that human nature, created in your image
and washed clean through the Sacrament of Baptism
from all the squalor of the life of old,
may be found worthy to rise to the life of newborn children
through water and the Holy Spirit.

And, if appropriate, lowering the paschal candle into the water either
once or three times, he continues:
May the power of the Holy Spirit,
O Lord, we pray,
come down through your Son
into the fullness of this font,
and, holding the candle in the water, he continues:
so that all who have been buried with Christ
by Baptism into death
may rise again to life with him.
Who lives and reigns with you in the unity of the Holy Spirit,
one God, for ever and ever.
R. Amen.

47 Then the candle is lifted out of the water, as the people acclaim:
Springs of water, bless the Lord;
praise and exalt him above all for ever.

The Blessing of Water

54 If no one present is to be baptized and the font is not to be blessed, the
Priest introduces the faithful to the blessing of water, saying:
Dear brothers and sisters,
let us humbly beseech the Lord our God
to bless this water he has created,
which will be sprinkled upon us
as a memorial of our Baptism.
May he graciously renew us,
that we may remain faithful to the Spirit
whom we have received.

And after a brief pause in silence, he proclaims the following prayer, with
hands extended:
Lord our God,
in your mercy be present to your people
who keep vigil on this most sacred night,
and, for us who recall the wondrous work of our creation
and the still greater work of our redemption,
graciously bless this water.
For you created water to make the fields fruitful
and to refresh and cleanse our bodies.
You also made water the instrument of your mercy:
for through water you freed your people from slavery
and quenched their thirst in the desert;
through water the Prophets proclaimed the new covenant
you were to enter upon with the human race;
and last of all,
through water, which Christ made holy in the Jordan,
you have renewed our corrupted nature
in the bath of regeneration.
Therefore, may this water be for us
a memorial of the Baptism we have received,
and grant that we may share
in the gladness of our brothers and sisters,
who at Easter have received their Baptism.
Through Christ our Lord.
R. Amen.

Reflection

Daily experience makes us very conscious that water cleanses, purifies, washes away all that stains and sullies. And yet one of the strongest images in the Church's baptismal tradition is that water also is creative; it brings about new life, causes new beginnings. Just as the Church is the mother of God's children, so too is the baptismal water, in the words of St. Cyril of Jerusalem (c. 318–386), "both tomb and mother."

Suggested Questions for Discussion

1   Should the presider sing the prayer over the water?

2   Is it better for the assembly to stand or sit during the blessing?

Celebration of Baptism – Profession of Faith

Historical Survey

Immediately prior to the Baptism itself comes the renunciation of sin, (in some countries the anointing with the oil of catechumens), and the profession of faith. Evidence of their antiquity is found in the early text known as the *Apostolic Tradition*.

> The priest will take aside each of those who are to receive baptism. He will order each to turn to the west and to make his abjuration in these words:
> **I renounce you, Satan,**
> **and all your undertakings and all your works.**
> *After this abjuration he anoints them with the oil of exorcism, saying:*
> **"Let every evil spirit depart from you."**
>
> *The person to be baptized lays aside his clothes [and] . . . goes down into the water. The one doing the baptizing lays his hand on him and asks him:*
> **Do you believe in God, the Father almighty?**
> *The one being baptized is to answer:*
> **"I believe."**
> *Let him baptize him a first time . . .*

The renunciation, a negative rite found in both East and West, assumed various forms, some being quite simple and others being more elaborate, either by means of questions and answers or simple declarative statements. The original focal point of the renunciation seems to have been the pagan deities and the manifestation of their worship in such events as theatrical spectacles, the circus, etc. In some places, for example, Rome, the candidates faced the west when renouncing the demons since the east was associated with Christ, the west being, as St. Gregory of Nyssa (c. 330–c. 395) called it, "the place where dwells the power of darkness."

The pre-baptismal anointing (in the United States omitted at the Paschal Vigil) was performed with what was called the oil of exorcism. The rite, done today with what is called the oil of the catechumens, appears to have had an exorcistic origin, healing and strengthening the body against its struggles with the devil. According to many of the ancient sources, this anointing signifies that the person to be baptized will share in Christ, who is the true olive (from which the oil is made).

As to the profession of faith, early on it was part of the water bath itself, assuming the form of a threefold series of questions and answers, each followed by a plunging into the water: e.g. "Do you believe in . . .?"

Documentation

Rite of Christian Initiation of Adults

211 RENUNCIATION OF SIN AND PROFESSION OF FAITH: In their renunciation of sin and profession of faith those to be baptized express their explicit faith in the paschal mystery that has already been recalled in the blessing of the water and that will be connoted by the words of the sacrament soon to be spoken by the baptizing minister. Adults are not saved unless they come forward of their own accord and with the will to accept God's gift through their own belief. The faith of those to be baptized is not simply the faith of the Church, but the personal faith of each one of them and each one of them is expected to keep it a living faith.

Therefore the renunciation of sin and the profession of faith are an apt prelude to baptism, the sacrament of that faith by which the elect hold fast to God and receive new birth from him. Because of the renunciation of sin and the profession of faith, which form the one rite, the elect will not be baptized merely passively but will receive this great sacrament with the active resolve to renounce error and to hold fast to God. By their own personal act in the rite of renouncing sin and professing the faith, the elect, was prefigured in the first covenant with the patriarchs, renounce sin and Satan in order to commit themselves for ever to the promise of the Savior and to the mystery of the Trinity. By professing their faith before the celebrant and the entire community, the elect express the intention, developed to maturity during the preceding periods of initiation, to enter into a new covenant with Christ. Thus these adults embrace the faith that through divine help the Church has handed down, and are baptized in that faith.

Roman Missal

48   After the blessing of baptismal water and the acclamation of the people, the Priest, standing, puts the prescribed questions to the adults and the parents or godparents of the children, as is set out in the respective Rites of the Roman Ritual, in order for them to make the required renunciation.

      If the anointing of the adults with the Oil of Catechumens has not taken place beforehand, as part of the immediately preparatory rites, it occurs at this moment.

49   Then the Priest questions the adults individually about the faith and, if there are children to be baptized, he requests the triple profession of faith from all the parents and godparents together, as is indicated in the respective Rites.

      Where many are to be baptized on this night, it is possible to arrange the rite so that, immediately after the response of those to be baptized and of the godparents and the parents, the Celebrant asks for and receives the renewal of baptismal promises of all present.

Reflection

As the daily newspapers and the evening TV news programs so vividly remind us, the powers of darkness and evil are alive in the world today. Yet both individual Christians as well as the whole community are called to "lay aside the works of darkness and put on the armor of light" (Rom 13:12). No longer living according to the "prince of this world" (Eph 2:2) we, by reason of Baptism which makes us sharers in the very life of Christ himself, continue to place our faith in God, to journey down the path of light, and always to seek the light that flows from God the Father through the Son and by means of the Holy Spirit.

Suggested Question for Discussion

1   Is it appropriate for the whole assembly to join the baptismal candidates in making the renunciation and the profession of faith?

Celebration of Baptism –
Baptism

Historical Survey

The *Didache*, one of the earliest Church documents (parts of the treatise perhaps date from the end of the first century), gives us a clue as to how people were baptized in the subapostolic Christian community.

> Baptize in the name of the Father and of the Son and of the Holy Spirit, doing so in running water. But if you have no running water, baptize in other water; if you cannot in cold water, then in warm water. But if you have neither, pour water three times on the head in the name of the Father and of the Son and of the Holy Spirit. (VII)

For many years Baptism by immersion, so wonderfully imaging Paul's understanding of Baptism as dying and rising with Christ, was preferred to the mere pouring of water over a person's head. We should, however, be cautious in believing that an individual's whole body was always placed underwater since there is evidence to suggest that the candidate stood knee-deep in the baptismal pool and the bishop poured water over the head or perhaps dipped the head into the water. In the Western Church immersion in one form or another continued to be the normal method of baptizing till the sixteenth century. Today it has once again become the preferred though not most practiced manner of celebrating the sacrament.

The words of Jesus, "Baptize all nations in the name of the Father, and of the Son, and of the Holy Spirit," were ritually carried out in two ways. In parts of the East (or at least in Antioch) there was the simple declarative formula "N. is baptized in the name of . . ." In Jerusalem and in parts of the west (Africa, Milan, Rome) there was the question, "Do you believe in God the Father . . .?" followed by an answer, which in turn was followed by a dipping or immersion into the water. This sequence was repeated three times, once for each person of the Trinity.

The single Trinitarian formula used today, "N., I baptize you . . ." with a single immersion or a triple pouring, originated in the East and spread to Europe by means of Spain in the sixth century.

Documentation

Rite of Christian Initiation of Adults

226 BAPTISM: Immediately after their profession of living faith in Christ's paschal mystery, the elect come forward and receive that mystery as expressed in the washing with water; thus once the elect have professed faith in the Father, Son, and Holy Spirit, invoked by the celebrant, the divine persons act so that those they have chosen receive divine adoption and become members of the people of God.

213 Therefore in the celebration of baptism the washing with water should take on its full importance as the sign of that mystical sharing in Christ's death and resurrection through which those who believe in his name should be chosen for the rite, whichever will serve in individual cases and in the various traditions and circumstances to ensure the clear understanding that this washing is not a mere purification rite but the sacrament of being joined to Christ.

Baptism

575 The celebrant baptizes each candidate either by immersion, option A, or by the pouring of water, option B. Each baptism may be followed by a short acclamation (Appendix II, no. 595), sung or said by the people.

[If there are a great number to be baptized, they may be divided into groups and baptized by assisting priests or deacons. In baptizing, either by immersion, option A, or by the pouring of water, option B, these ministers say the sacramental formulary for each candidate. During the baptisms, singing by the people is desirable or readings from Scripture or simply silent prayer.]

A If baptism is by immersion, of the whole body or of the head only, decency and decorum should be preserved. Either or both godparents touch the candidate. The celebrant, immersing the candidate's whole body or head three times, baptizes the candidate in the name of the Trinity.
N., I baptize you in the name of the Father,
He immerses the candidate the first time.
and of the Son,
He immerses the candidate the second time.
and of the Holy Spirit.
He immerses the candidate the third time.

B If baptism is by the pouring of water, either or both godparents place the right hand on the shoulder of the candidate, and the celebrant, taking baptismal water and pouring it three times on the candidate's bowed head, baptize the candidate in the name of the Trinity.

N., I baptize you in the name of the Father,
He pours water the first time.
and of the Son,
He pours water the second time.
and of the Holy Spirit.
He pours water the third time.

National Statutes for the Catechumenate

17 Baptism by immersion is the fuller and more expressive sign of the sacrament and, therefore provision should be made for its more frequent use in the baptism of adults. At the least, the provision of the *Rite of Christian Initiation of Adults* for partial immersion, namely, immersion of the candidate's head, should be taken into account.

Roman Missal

50 When the interrogation is concluded, the Priest baptizes the adult elect and the children.

Reflection

To baptize is not merely a utilitarian action nor a sign with restricted meaning. Akin to the Eucharist itself, Baptism is in its deepest sense a multi-faceted reality, a sacrament having meaning on several levels. It is, according to the Lord's command, to share in the very life of the Trinity and to enjoy a unique relationship with each person of that Trinity. It is to have joined Christ in struggling against and overcoming the powers of darkness and alienation. It is to have come up from Christ's three-day burial in the tomb to join him in his bodily resurrection, which itself is a sign and a pledge of the resurrection of our own bodies at the end of the world.

Suggested Questions for Discussion

1 Why is immersion the preferred method of baptizing?

2 If immersion is used, what practical details need be attended to?

3 What possible motifs might a post-baptismal acclamation have?

Celebration of Baptism – Explanatory Rites, Anointing with Oil

Historical Survey

In third-century Rome the newly baptized, upon emerging from the baptismal pool, were anointed with the "oil of thanksgiving" as one of the priests assisting the bishop said: "I anoint you with holy oil in the name of Jesus Christ." This anointing, upon the head and eventually made with the sign of the cross, came to be understood as symbolizing the neophyte's membership among Christ's elect. Just as in the Old Testament the priest, prophet, and king were anointed, so does the new Christian share in the priestly, prophetic, and royal mission of Christ.

Documentation

Rite of Christian Initiation of Adults

214 The baptismal washing is followed by rites that give expression to the effects of the sacrament just received. The anointing with chrism is a sign of the royal priesthood of the baptized and that they are now numbered in the company of the people of God. . .

227 The celebration of baptism continues with the explanatory rites, after which the celebration of confirmation normally follows.

Anointing after Baptism

228 If the confirmation of those baptized is separated from their baptism, the celebrant anoints them with chrism immediately after baptism.
[When a great number have been baptized, assisting priests or deacons may help with the anointing.]
The celebrant first says the following over all the newly baptized before the anointing.
The God of power and the Father of our Lord Jesus Christ
has freed you from sin
and brought you to new life through water and the Holy Spirit.
He now anoints you with the chrism of salvation,
so that united with his people,
you may remain for ever a member of Christ
who is Priest, Prophet, and King.
Newly baptized: Amen.

In silence each of the newly baptized is anointed with chrism on the crown of the head.

National Statutes for the Catechumenate
16 The rite of anointing with the oil of catechumens is to be omitted in the baptism of adults at the Easter Vigil.

Roman Missal
51 After the Baptism, the Priest anoints the infants with chrism.

Reflection

"Christian is my name, and Catholic my surname. The one designates me, whereas the other makes me specific. Thus I am attested and set apart." (*St. Pacian of Barcelona [d. 379–392]*).

Suggested Question for Discussion

1   Why is this anointing ordinarily omitted at the Baptism of adults during the Easter Vigil?

Celebration of Baptism – Explanatory Rites, Clothing with a Baptismal Garment

Historical Survey

In the early Church those to be baptized first laid aside their clothing before going down into the pool (thus the need for deaconesses to assist the women). Then, after the water bath, they put on white garments. St. Ambrose (c.339–397) explained the meaning of them as a "sign that you have taken off the clothing of sin and that you have been clad in the pure garments of innocence" (*On the Mysteries* 34). The old garments, according to the thought of St. Paul (Col 3:9), thus stood for what was called the "old self," the new clothing symbolizing the "new self."

In many areas this white garment, a sign of baptismal innocence and newness, was worn throughout Easter week, which Asterius (d. after 341) called "the shining week." This special clothing was removed on the Sunday after Easter, a day known as the *dominica in [depositis] albis*, namely, the Sunday on which the white garments were removed.

In many places the garment eventually became a "white linen cloth" (at least for infants), a good example of a sign taking the place of another sign or symbol. Today's rite, in a spirit of authenticity, calls for a "garment."

Documentation

Rite of Christian Initiation of Adults

214B The clothing with the baptismal garment signifies the new dignity [the newly baptized] have received.

Clothing with a Baptismal Garment

229 The garment used in this rite may be white or of a color that conforms to local custom. If circumstances suggest, this rite may be omitted.

The celebrant says the following formulary, and at the words "Receive this baptismal garment" the godparents place the garment on the newly baptized.
N. and N., you have become a new creation
and have clothed yourselves in Christ.
Receive this baptismal garment
and bring it unstained to the judgment seat
of our Lord Jesus Christ,
so that you may have everlasting life.
Newly baptized. Amen.

Roman Missal

51 A white garment is given to each, whether adults or children.

BCL Newsletter

In recent months the Secretariat for the Liturgy has received several inquiries concerning the baptismal garment for adults. The common practice in the dioceses of this country is to use an alb or other white garment, though the practice of using a colored garment or even a chasuble or dalmatic has begun to appear in some places. The Rite of Christian Initiation of Adults describes the optional clothing of the neophyte with the baptismal garment immediately following baptism. The garment is described as white or some other color according to local custom (RCIA 220). The General Instruction of the Roman Missal is quite clear that since vesture symbolizes the function of the one who wears it (GIRM 297), the chasuble is reserved for priests and the dalmatic for deacons

(299, 230). Other ministers may wear albs or, by local custom, the cassock and surplice.

Thus it would seem that the most appropriate vesture for neophytes would be a white garment, probably in the shape of an alb or choir robe. If a baptismal garment is not specially created, an alb or white choir robe could appropriately be used. In no instance should those who are not ordained be vested in chasuble, stole or dalmatic.

Reflection

As Christians we not only have roots in the past and live in the present, but we are also future-oriented, for to be a Christian is to look forward to a glory that has already begun, yet will achieve its full measure when Christ comes again in glory. The life to come will be a life without end; it is a life we already possess in Christ. It is a life that as of now has begun.

Suggested Questions for Discussion

1   Who should make the baptismal garment?

2   What should be its dimensions for infants? Adults?

3   Some communities use small "stoles" for infants. Good or bad idea and why?

4   Should the garment be worn during Easter week? On the Sunday after Easter?

5   What should happen to the garment after Easter?

Celebration of Baptism – Explanatory Rites, Presentation of a Lighted Candle

Historical Survey

The giving of a lighted candle to the newly baptized seems to have originated in the East where it was already described by Proclus of Constantinople (d. 446 or

447). The custom spread to Gaul and then to Rome where it appeared in the twelfth century papal liturgy. Medieval commentators often used the parable of the ten virgins to explain the symbolism of this rite.

Documentation

Rite of Christian Initiation of Adults

214C The presentation of a lighted candle shows that [the newly baptized] are called to walk as befits the children of light.

Presentation of a Lighted Candle

230 The celebrant takes the Easter candle in his hands or touches it, saying to the godparents:
Godparents, please come forward to give the newly baptized the light of Christ.

A godparent of each of the newly baptized goes to the celebrant, lights a candle from the Easter candle, then presents it to the newly baptized. Then the celebrant says to the newly baptized:
You have been enlightened by Christ.
Walk always as children of the light
and keep the flame of faith alive in your hearts.
When the Lord comes, may you go out to meet him
with all the saints in the heavenly kingdom.
Newly baptized: Amen.

Roman Missal

51 Then the Priest or Deacon receives the paschal candle from the hand of the minister, and the candles of the newly baptized are lighted. For infants the rite of Ephphetha is omitted.

52 Afterwards, unless the baptismal washing and the other explanatory rites have occurred in the sanctuary, a procession returns to the sanctuary, formed as before, with the newly baptized or the godparents or parents carrying lighted candles. During this procession, the baptismal canticle *Vidi aquam* (I saw water) or another appropriate chant is sung (no. 56).

Reflection

Baptism — like its counterpart, the Eucharist — is not just an action whereby we receive something. Rather, to have been baptized means to have been transformed, to have been changed into a new and glorious person. In the words of

St. Bernard of Clairvaux (1090–1153): "It is given to us all alike to catch the glory of the Lord in a mirror with faces unveiled; and so we become transfigured into the same likeness, borrowing glory from that glory, as the spirit of the Lord enables us."

Suggested Questions for Discussion

1   What happens to the candle after its presentation? After the Vigil?

Celebration of Confirmation

Historical Survey

It is in the Acts of the Apostles that we find our first witness to what we call today the sacrament of Confirmation. The Apostles Peter and John went to Samaria and prayed for those who had already been baptized "that they may receive the Holy Spirit . . . then they laid their hands on them, and they received the Holy Spirit" (Acts 8:14–17).

The manner in which this giving of the Holy Spirit developed in succeeding centuries has given rise to one of the most complex chapters in the history of the sacraments. We need only point out the early treatise, the *Apostolic Tradition*, once attributed to Hippolytus of Rome. Here the pattern of initiation, for both adults and infants, proceeded along a continuum having three principal moments. First there was the water bath carried out by the priests (assisted by deacons and in some areas deaconesses). Then, according to Hippolytus:

> . . . the bishop shall lay his hand upon them invoking and saying: O Lord God, you counted these worthy of deserving the forgiveness of sins by the bath of regeneration. Make them worthy to be filled with the Holy Spirit and send your grace upon them that they may serve you according to your will. To you is the glory, to the Father and to the Son . . .
>
> After pouring the consecrated oil and laying his land on his head, he shall say: I anoint you with holy oil in God the Father Almighty and Christ Jesus and the Holy Spirit. And sealing him on the forehead, he shall give him the kiss of peace . . .

Then all the newly baptized were "eucharistized," that is, they received the consecrated bread and wine.

But once it became customary for infants to be baptized shortly after birth, these babies had to wait for the episcopal rites of the imposition of hands and the anointing. In rural areas it could be a number of months or even years before the bishop would visit and confer the episcopal rites. In addition, the first reception of communion itself was delayed, thus becoming more and more separated from the Baptism itself. As a consequence the initiation pattern evolved from a ritual continuum of "baptism, confirmation, eucharist" to three separate liturgies, one for Baptism, one for first Eucharist, and a third for Confirmation, for both adults and non-adults. Whereas the eastern rites have always opted for the classic initiatory pattern (with "chrismation" always given immediately after the water bath and conferred by a priest using oil blessed by the bishop), the Roman Church preserved the immediate link between Confirmation and the bishop.

The Second Vatican Council's *Constitution on the Liturgy* (art. 71) requested that the "rite of confirmation . . . be revised in order that the intimate connection of this sacrament with the whole of Christian initiation may stand out more clearly . . ." When the revised Rite of Confirmation appeared in 1971, it gave the faculty to confirm to priests who, in virtue of an office they lawfully hold, baptize an adult or a child old enough to receive catechesis or receive a validly baptized adult into the full communion of the Church (*Rite of Confirmation* no. 7).

Documentation

Rite of Christian Initiation of Adults

215 In accord with the ancient practice followed in the Roman liturgy, adults are not to be baptized without receiving confirmation immediately afterward, unless some serious reason stands in the way. The conjunction of the two celebrations signifies the unity of the paschal mystery, the close link between the mission of the Son and the outpouring of the Holy Spirit, and the connection between the two sacraments through which the Son and the Holy Spirit come with the Father to those who are baptized.

216 Accordingly, confirmation is conferred after the explanatory rites of baptism, the anointing after baptism (no. 228) being omitted.

231 Between the celebration of baptism and confirmation, the congregation may sing a suitable song.

The place for the celebration of confirmation is either at the baptismal font or in the sanctuary, depending on the place where, according to local custom, baptism has been celebrated.

232   If the bishop has conferred baptism, he should now also confer confirmation. If the bishop is not present, the priest who conferred baptism is authorized to confirm.

[When there are a great many persons to be confirmed, the minister of confirmation may associate priests with himself as ministers of the sacrament (see no. 14).]

Invitation

233   The celebrant first speaks briefly to the newly baptized in these or similar words:
My dear newly baptized, born again in Christ by baptism, you have become members of Christ and of his priestly people. Now you are to share in the outpouring of the Holy Spirit among us, the Spirit sent by the Lord upon his apostles at Pentecost and given by them and their successors to the baptized.

The promised strength of the Holy Spirit, which you are to receive, will make you more like Christ and help you to be witnesses to his suffering, death, and resurrection. It will strengthen you to be active members of the Church and to build up the Body of Christ in faith and love.
[The priests who will be associated with the celebrant as ministers of the sacrament now stand next to him.]
With hands joined, the celebrant next addresses the people:
My dear friends, let us pray to God our Father, that he will pour out the Holy Spirit on these newly baptized to strengthen them with his gifts and anoint them to be more like Christ, the Son of God.

All pray briefly in silence.

Laying on of Hands

234   The celebrant holds his hands outstretched over the entire group of those to be confirmed and says the following prayer.
[In silence the priests associated as ministers of the sacrament also hold their hands outstretched over the candidates.]
All-powerful God, Father of our Lord Jesus Christ,
by water and the Holy Spirit
you freed your sons and daughters from sin
and gave them new life.
Send your Holy Spirit upon them
to be their helper and guide.
Give them the spirit of wisdom and understanding,
the spirit of right judgment and courage,

the spirit of knowledge and reverence.
Fill them with the spirit of wonder and awe in your presence.
We ask this through Christ our Lord.
R. Amen.

Anointing with Chrism

235 A minister brings the chrism to the celebrant.

[When the celebrant is the bishop, priests who are associated as ministers of the sacrament receive the chrism from him.]

Each candidate, with godparent or godparents or with sponsors, goes to the celebrant (or to an associated minister of the sacrament); or, if circumstances require, the celebrant (associated ministers) may go to the candidates.

Either or both godparents and sponsors place the right hand on the shoulder of the candidate; a godparent or a sponsor or the candidate gives the candidate's name to the minister of the sacrament. During the conferral of the sacrament an appropriate song may be sung.

The minister of the sacrament dips his right thumb in the chrism and makes the sign of the cross on the forehead of the one to be confirmed as he says:
N., be sealed with the Gift of the Holy Spirit.
Newly confirmed: Amen.
The minister of the sacrament adds:
Peace be with you.
Newly confirmed: And also with you.

After all have received the sacrament, the newly confirmed as well as the godparents and sponsors are led to their places in the assembly.

Roman Missal

53 If adults have been baptized, the Bishop or, in his absence, the Priest who has conferred Baptism, should at once administer the Sacrament of Confirmation to them in the sanctuary, as is indicated in the Roman Pontifical or Roman Ritual.

Reflection

One characteristic of modern life, including our lives as Christians, is a tendency to put things into neat little boxes, namely, to compartmentalize. All too often we view our faith journey as consisting of isolated stages, each having a beginning or an end. And so the sacraments are also viewed as individual ritual actions, celebrated no matter when and without any internal relationship to one another. We forget, for example, that ordination to the priesthood is closely connected to Baptism. Something similar is also true of the pattern of initiation where it is not a question of one sacrament versus another sacrament, but of sacramental unity, of a sacramental "economy." As to Confirmation, one author put it ever so well when he wrote: "Confirmation is not a reaffirmation of a previous baptism. . . . It is, rather, the gift of the Spirit tied intimately to the water-bath that prepares one for the reception of the body and blood of Christ as a full member of the church" (Gerard Austin, *The Rite of Confirmation: Anointing with the Spirit*, p. 146).

Suggested Questions for Discussion

1   What is the purpose of the optional hymn before the celebration of Confirmation?

2   How does the "principle of liberality" apply in regard to Confirmation?

3   If a song is sung during the Confirmation itself, when should it, namely, the song, begin? What should be its theme?

4   Who will lead the newly confirmed and their godparents and sponsors back to their places in the assembly?

Renewal of Baptismal Promises

Historical Survey

In Rome on Easter evening the newly baptized were accustomed to gather and pray at the baptistery where they had undergone the water bath the previous night, thereby recalling what they had experienced during their Baptism. Such forms of baptismal memorials have long been common in Christianity. In a number of old liturgical books we find prayers — called the *pascha annotina* ("last year's Easter") — said by the priest on the annual anniversary of a person's Baptism. This reminds us of the present-day injunction that newly baptized adults gather one year later for prayer, reflection, and mutual support (see RCIA no. 250). Additional reminders of our Baptism are the baptismal candle, the use of holy water, and the Sunday sprinkling of the gathered assembly.

During the Easter Vigil the people renew their baptismal commitment by means of a renunciation of sin (with two options for the formula to be used), followed by a profession of faith and a sprinkling accompanied by the singing of the "I saw water" ("*Vidi aquam*") or a similar text. This water rite, originating in monasteries as a purification ritual, soon took on the baptismal character it has today.

Documentation

Circular Letter "Paschalis sollemnitatis"

89 Next follows the renewal of baptismal promises, introduced by some words on the part of the celebrating priest. The faithful reply to the questions put to them, standing and holding lighted candles in their hands. They are then sprinkled with water: in this way the gestures and words remind them of the Baptism they have received. The celebrating priest sprinkles the people by passing through the main part of the church while all sing the antiphon "*Vidi aquam*" or another suitable song of a baptismal character.

Roman Missal

The Renewal of Baptismal Promises

55 When the Rite of Baptism (and Confirmation) has been completed or, if this has not taken place, after the blessing of water, all stand, holding lighted candles in their hands, and renew the promise of baptismal faith, unless this has already been done together with those to be baptized (cf. no. 49).

The Priest addresses the faithful in these or similar words:
Dear brethren (brothers and sisters), through the Paschal Mystery
we have been buried with Christ in Baptism,
so that we may walk with him in newness of life.
And so, now that our Lenten observance is concluded,
let us renew the promises of Holy Baptism,
by which we once renounced Satan and his works
and promised to serve God in the holy Catholic Church.
And so I ask you:
Priest: Do you renounce Satan?
All: I do.
Priest: And all his works?

All: I do.
Priest: And all his empty show?
All: I do.
Or:
Priest: Do you renounce sin,
so as to live in the freedom of the children of God?
All: I do.
Priest: Do you renounce the lure of evil,
so that sin may have no mastery over you?
All: I do.
Priest: Do you renounce Satan, the author and prince of sin?
All: I do.
If the situation warrants, this second formula may be adapted by Conferences of Bishops according to local needs.
Then the Priest continues:
Priest: Do you believe in God, the Father almighty,
Creator of heaven and earth?
All: I do.
Priest: Do you believe in Jesus Christ, his only Son, our Lord,
who was born of the Virgin Mary, suffered death and was buried,
rose again from the dead, and is seated at the right hand of the Father?
All: I do.
Priest: Do you believe in the Holy Spirit, the holy Catholic Church,
the communion of saints, the forgiveness of sins,
the resurrection of the body, and life everlasting?
All: I do.
And the Priest concludes:
And may almighty God, the Father of our Lord Jesus Christ,
who has given us new birth by water and the Holy Spirit
and bestowed on us forgiveness of our sins,
keep us by his grace,
in Christ Jesus our Lord, for eternal life.
All: Amen.

56   The Priest sprinkles the people with the blessed water, while all sing:
      Vidi Aquam
      Ant. I saw water flowing from the Temple,
      from its right-hand side, alleluia;
      and all to whom this water came were saved
      and shall say: Alleluia, alleluia.
      Another chant that is baptismal in character may also be sung.

57   Meanwhile the newly baptized are led to their place among the faithful.

      If the blessing of baptismal water has not taken place in the baptistery, the
      Deacon and the ministers reverently carry the vessel of water to the font.

If the blessing of the font has not occurred, the blessed water is put aside in an appropriate place.

58 After the sprinkling, the Priest returns to the chair where, omitting the Creed, he directs the Universal Prayer, in which the newly baptized participate for the first time.

Reflection

Most Christians, having been baptized as infants, possess no living memory of having been baptized. As a result, a number of Protestant churches have long incorporated a renewal of baptismal vows into their liturgical calendars. Yet it was only in the 1951 revision of the Easter Vigil that such a baptismal renewal was adopted by the Roman Church. Nonetheless, the bottom line is not what we say in ritual form, as important as this is. What is important is that we live in accord with what we profess. One of the *pascha annotina* prayers expresses this ever so well: "Grant that . . . what we relive in memory we may always put into action."

Suggested Questions for Discussion

1 What can be done to link this renewal of promises with the profession of faith made earlier by the candidates?

2 Who lights the candles held by the members of the assembly?

3 Do these candle-lighters need instruction on how to light these candles?

4 Some have suggested that the peace be exchanged after the sprinkling rite. Good idea or bad idea?

Celebration of Reception

Historical Survey

During the third century the Church was faced with many problems, some theological, some of a practical nature, others being a combination of both. An example of the latter was the dispute, often quite bitter, regarding Baptism conferred by heretics. Was it a "true" Baptism or not? Did it need to be repeated? The Church in Africa as well as various churches in the East considered such baptisms to be invalid and thus "rebaptized." Rome and Alexandria, on the other hand, deemed these baptisms to be valid and merely required that those coming from heretical sects be, in some form or another, reconciled. A true Baptism, no matter the faith stance of the person conferring it, was not to be repeated, a principle found in the 1967 *Roman Ecumenical Directory*: "baptism . . . can be conferred only once."

During the years subsequent to the Reformation converts from Protestantism, whose former baptisms were judged valid, usually met with a priest in a private ceremony, often in a church. Kneeling before him, the convert recited a profession of faith which included an adherence to a long listing of articles denied by the Reformers. Today this ceremony of reception is a simple one; words are relatively few; the rite, however, is a public one.

The Rite of Christian Initiation of Adults contains a ceremony for receiving the already baptized into the full communion of the Catholic Church and states that "the rite should ordinarily take place within Mass" (RCIA no. 475). Also included is a rite for celebrating this reception after the celebration of Baptism during the Vigil (RCIA nos. 562–594); the decision should be guided by pastoral considerations, and so such a combined celebration is not an ordinary liturgical pattern. So it is that the National Conference of Catholic Bishops' 1988 *National Statutes for the Catechumenate* state that preferably this reception into full communion not take place during the Vigil.

In such a combined celebration the reception into full communion follows the explanatory baptismal rites; afterwards occurs the Confirmation followed by the renewal of the baptismal promises.

Documentation

Rite of Christian Initiation of Adults: Appendix I

4   Celebration at the Easter Vigil of the Sacraments of Initiation
and of the Rite of Reception
into the Full Communion of the Catholic Church

The Father chose us in Christ to be holy and spotless in love

562 Pastoral considerations may suggest that along with the celebration of the sacraments of Christian initiation the Easter Vigil should include the rite of reception of already baptized Christians into the full communion of the Catholic Church. But such a decision must be guided by the theological and pastoral directives proper to each rite. The model provided here simply arranges the ritual elements belonging to such a combined celebration. But the

model can only be used properly in the light of nos. 206–217, regarding celebration of the sacraments of Christian initiation, and of nos. 473–486, regarding the rite of reception into the full communion of the Catholic Church.

563 Inclusion at the Easter Vigil of the rite of reception into full communion may also be opportune liturgically, especially when the candidates have undergone a lengthy period of spiritual formation coinciding with Lent. In the liturgical year the Easter Vigil, the preeminent commemoration of Christ's paschal mystery, is the preferred occasion for the celebration in which the elect will enter the paschal mystery through baptism, confirmation, and Eucharist. Candidates for reception, who in baptism have already been justified by faith and incorporated into Christ, are entering fully into a community that is constituted by its communion both in faith and in the sacramental sharing of the paschal mystery. The celebration of their reception at the Easter Vigil provides the candidates with a privileged opportunity to recall and reaffirm their own baptism, "the sacramental bond of unity [and] foundation of communion between all Christians." At the Easter Vigil these candidates can make their baptismal profession of faith by joining the community in the renewal of the baptismal promises, and, if they have not yet been confirmed, they can receive the sacrament of confirmation, which is intimately connected with baptism. Since of its nature baptism points to complete entrance into Eucharistic communion, the baptismal themes of the Easter Vigil can serve to emphasize why the high point of the candidates' reception is their sharing in the Eucharist with the Catholic community for the first time (see 475.1).

564 The decision to combine the two celebrations at the Easter Vigil must be guided by the provision in the *Rite of Reception*, Introduction (no. 475.2). The decision should, then, be consistent in the actual situation with respect for ecumenical values and be guided by attentiveness both to local conditions and to personal and family preferences. The person to be received should always be consulted about the form of reception (see no. 475.2).

565 In its actual arrangement the celebration must reflect the status of candidates for reception into the full communion of the Catholic Church: such candidates have already been incorporated into Christ in baptism and anything that would equate them with catechumens is to be absolutely avoided (see no. 477).

584 If baptism has been celebrated at the font, the celebrant, the assisting ministers, and the newly baptized with their godparents, proceed to the sanctuary. As they do so the assembly may sing a suitable song.

Then in the following or similar words the celebrant invites the candidates for reception, along with their sponsors, to come into the sanctuary and before the community to make a profession of faith.
N. and N., of your own free will you have asked to be received
into the full communion of the Catholic Church.
You have made your decision after careful thought
under the guidance of the Holy Spirit.
I now invite you to come forward with your sponsors
and in the presence of this community to profess the Catholic faith.
In this faith you will be one with us for the first time
at the Eucharistic table of the Lord Jesus,
the sign of the Church's unity.

Profession by the Candidates

585 When the candidates for reception and their sponsors have taken their places in the sanctuary, the celebrant asks the candidates to make the following profession of faith. The candidates say:
I believe and profess all that the holy Catholic Church
believes, teaches, and proclaims to be revealed by God.

Act of Reception

586 Then the candidates with their sponsors go individually to the celebrant, who says to each candidate (laying his right hand on the head of any candidate who is not to receive confirmation):
N., the Lord receives you into the Catholic Church.
His loving kindness has led you here,
so that in the unity of the Holy Spirit
you may have full communion with us
in the faith that you have professed in the presence of his family.

National Statutes for the Catechumenate

30 Those who have already been baptized in another Church or ecclesial community should not be treated as catechumens or so designated. Their doctrinal and spiritual preparation for reception into full Catholic communion should be determined according to the individual case, that is, it should depend on the extent to which the baptized person has led a Christian life within a community of faith and been appropriately catechized to deepen his or her inner adherence to the Church.

32 The reception of candidates into the communion of the Catholic Church should ordinarily take place at the Sunday Eucharist of the parish community, in such a way that it is understood that they are indeed Christian believers who have already shared in the sacramental life of the Church and are now welcomed into the Catholic eucharistic community upon their profession of faith and confirmation, if they have not been confirmed, before receiving the eucharist.

33 It is preferable that reception into full communion not take place at the Easter Vigil lest there be any confusion of such baptized Christians with the candidates for baptism, possible misunderstanding of or even reflection upon the sacrament of baptism celebrated in another Church or ecclesial community, or any perceived triumphalism in the liturgical welcome into the Catholic eucharistic community.

34 Nevertheless if there are both catechumens to be baptized and baptized Christians to be received into full communion at the Vigil, for pastoral reasons and in view of the Vigil's being the principal annual celebration of the Church, the combined rite is to be followed: "Celebration at the Easter Vigil of the Sacraments of Initiation and of the Rite of Reception into the Full Communion of the Catholic Church." A clear distinction should be maintained during the celebration between candidates for sacramental initiation and candidates for reception into full communion, and ecumenical sensitivities should be carefully respected.

Reflection

Certainly as Roman Catholics we share much, in terms of dogma or theology, with many members of the Protestant churches. Together we believe in the Trinity, God's creative power on behalf of the human race, the need for reconciliation, the centrality of Christ and his saving mission, etc. Yet basic to such foundational unity is the sacrament of Baptism. So it is that some might argue that the Catholic assembly does well to welcome during the Vigil those individuals who, baptized in other denominations, make further progress on their journey to God's kingdom. And by the same token it is during this night that the Roman Church also acknowledges and honors the baptismal bond it shares with other Christian Churches. On the other hand, as the *National Statutes for the Catechumenate* so well state, there are compelling reasons for not celebrating this combining of rites. The question is what might be the pastoral reasons for celebrating both Baptism and reception together at the Easter Vigil? It is a question demanding serious reflection, not "we did it last year."

Suggested Questions for Discussion

1   What "pastoral reasons," if any, might suggest having the reception into full Catholic communion during the Easter Vigil?

2   If celebrated, what dangers are to be avoided?

Liturgy of the Eucharist

Historical Survey

For the early Church in Rome, as well as for us today, the third moment of a neophyte's initiation into the Church was that part of the liturgy when the newly baptized and confirmed received the Lord's Eucharistic body and blood. And just as the baptismal rite itself was expanded by other rites, the same was true in some localities for the communion. In both Africa and Rome milk and honey were given to the new Christians as well as, in Rome, a cup containing water (symbolizing purification). Hippolytus relates that the cup with the milk and honey had a threefold meaning, signifying: the neophytes like the Jews of old passing through the waters to the promised land flowing with milk and honey; the Eucharist being akin to the food little children eat; the milk and honey symbolizing the sweetness of God's word, which makes gentle the human heart. Some speculate that the use of milk and honey may have originated in Jewish-Christian communities.

Today the Church strongly recommends that the neophytes take part in the procession of the gifts. Such was not always the case. Although no evidence from Rome makes no mention of them doing so, St. Ambrose (c. 339–397) reproved such a practice, saying — and rather unconvincingly — that only mature Christians might participate in this procession (and yet the newly initiated were allowed access to the Eucharist?).

For centuries, the Easter Vigil Mass lacked certain standard structural elements (no offertory chant, no exchange of peace, no *Agnus Dei*, no communion song), either a sign of the antiquity of the Vigil Mass or the result of a time when people in general did not receive the Eucharist during the celebration, which itself was gradually being moved forward to Saturday afternoon or earlier.

Today the Eucharist celebrated during the Easter Vigil has pride of place among all the Church's celebrations of praise and thanksgiving. It is the Easter Eucharist.

Documentation

Circular Letter "Paschalis sollemnitatis"

90 The celebration of the Eucharist forms the fourth part of the Vigil and marks its high point, for it is in the fullest sense the Easter Sacrament, that is to say, the commemoration of the Sacrifice of the Cross and the presence of the risen Christ, the completion of Christian initiation, and the foretaste of the eternal pasch.

91 Great care should be taken that this Eucharistic Liturgy is not celebrated in haste. Indeed, all the rites and words must be given their full force: the General Intercessions in which for the first time the neophytes now as members of the faithful exercise their priesthood; the procession at the offertory in which the neophytes, if there are any, take part; the first, second or third Eucharistic Prayer, preferably sung, with its proper embolisms; and finally, Eucharistic Communion, as the moment of full participation in the mystery that is being celebrated. It is appropriate that at Communion there be sung Psalm 117 with the antiphon "*Pascha nostrum*," or Psalm 33 with the antiphon "Alleluia, alleluia, alleluia," or some other song of Easter exultation.

92 It is fitting that in the Communion of the Easter Vigil full expression be given to the symbolism of the Eucharist, namely by consuming the Eucharist under the species of both bread and wine. The local Ordinaries will consider the appropriateness of such a concession and its ramifications.

Rite of Christian Initiation of Adults

217 Finally in the celebration of the Eucharist, as they take part for the first time and with full right, the newly baptized reach the culminating point in their Christian initiation. In this Eucharist the neophytes, now raised to the ranks of the royal priesthood, have an active part both in the general intercessions and, to the extent possible, in bringing the gifts to the altar. With the entire community they share in the offering of the sacrifice and say the Lord's Prayer, giving expression to the spirit of adoption as God's children that they have received in baptism. When in communion they receive the body that was given for us and the blood that was shed, the neophytes are strengthened in the gifts they have already received and are given a foretaste of the eternal banquet.

243 It is most desirable that the neophytes, together with their godparents, sponsors, parents, spouses, and catechists, receive communion under both kinds.

449 . . . Some of the neophytes also take part in the procession to the altar with the gifts.

Roman Missal

Fourth Part:
The Liturgy of the Eucharist

59 The Priest goes to the altar and begins the Liturgy of the Eucharist in the usual way.

60 It is desirable that the bread and wine be brought forward by the newly baptized or, if they are children, by their parents or godparents.

61 **Prayer over the Offerings**
Accept, we ask, O Lord,
the prayers of your people
with the sacrificial offerings,
that what has begun in the paschal mysteries
may, by the working of your power,
bring us to the healing of eternity.
Through Christ our Lord.

62 Preface I of Easter: The Paschal Mystery (. . . on this night above all . . .).

63 In the Eucharistic Prayer, a commemoration is made of the baptized and their godparents in accord with the formulas which are found in the Roman Missal and Roman Ritual for each of the Eucharistic Prayers.

64 Before the *Ecce Agnus Dei* (Behold the Lamb of God), the Priest may briefly address the newly baptized about receiving their first Communion and about the excellence of this great mystery, which is the climax of Initiation and the center of the whole of Christian life.

65 It is desirable that the newly baptized receive Holy Communion under both kinds, together with their godfathers, godmothers, and Catholic parents and spouses, as well as their lay catechists. It is even appropriate that, with the consent of the Diocesan Bishop, where the occasion suggests this, all the faithful be admitted to Holy Communion under both kinds.

66 **Communion Antiphon** I Cor 5: 7–8
Christ our Passover has been sacrificed;
therefore let us keep the feast
with the unleavened bread of purity and truth, alleluia.

Psalm 118 (117) may appropriately be sung.

67 **Prayer after Communion**
Pour out on us, O Lord, the Spirit of your love,
and in your kindness make those you have nourished
by this paschal Sacrament
one in mind and heart.
Through Christ our Lord.

68 **Solemn Blessing**
May almighty God bless you
through today's Easter Solemnity
and, in his compassion,
defend you from every assault of sin.
R. Amen.
And may he, who restores you to eternal life
in the Resurrection of his Only Begotten,
endow you with the prize of immortality.
R. Amen.
Now that the days of the Lord's Passion have drawn to a close,
may you who celebrate the gladness of the Paschal Feast
come with Christ's help, and exulting in spirit,
to those feasts that are celebrated in eternal joy.
R. Amen.
And may the blessing of almighty God,
the Father, and the Son, ✠ and the Holy Spirit,
come down on you and remain with you for ever.
R. Amen.

The final blessing formula from the Rite of Baptism of Adults or of Children may also be used, according to circumstances.

69 To dismiss the people the Deacon or, if there is no Deacon, the Priest himself sings or says:
Go forth, the Mass is ended, alleluia, alleluia.
Or:
Go in peace, alleluia, alleluia.
All reply
Thanks be to God, alleluia, alleluia.

This practice is observed throughout the Octave of Easter.

211 Night Prayer for Holy Saturday is said only by those who are not present at the Easter Vigil.

Reflection

In light of the very length of the Vigil and the energy and attention devoted to preparing and celebrating the Solemn Beginning of the Vigil, the Liturgy of the Word, and the Baptismal Liturgy, there is the danger of viewing the Liturgy of the Eucharist as merely an appendage to the celebration. And yet it is toward the Eucharist that all has been progressing, for the Eucharist is the very culmination of the night's festivities. Tonight's Eucharist is the "Easter sacrament paramount."

Suggested Questions for Discussion

1   Who should present the gifts?

2   In some communities the candles held by the members of the assembly remain lighted till the end of the Eucharistic prayer. Good idea or bad idea?

3   Should the first communion of the newly baptized be especially highlighted? If so, how?

4   Why is communion under both kinds to be especially encouraged?

5   Might of the blessing of foods take place in conjunction with the Eucharistic liturgy? If so, when?

THE MASS
DURING THE DAY
(EASTER SUNDAY)

The Mass During the Day
(Easter Sunday)

Introductory Rites

LITURGY OF THE WORD
First Reading
Psalm Response
Second Reading
Sequence
Gospel Acclamation
Gospel
Homily
Renewal of Baptismal Promises (In the United States)
General Intercessions

LITURGY OF THE EUCHARIST
Preparation Rite
Eucharistic Prayer
Communion Rite
Solemn Prayer
or
Prayer over the People and Dismissal

The Mass During the Day

Historical Survey

Originally no special Mass was celebrated on this Sunday since the Easter celebration was the Vigil itself which began on Holy Saturday evening and concluded during the early hours of Sunday. And yet traces of a further Easter celebration can be found in Jerusalem at the end of the fourth century, in Africa at the beginning of the fifth century, and in Rome at the turn of the sixth century.

Why such a development? Perhaps to prolong the spirit of the evening or night celebration, which, nonetheless, went on till Pentecost Sunday. Perhaps to accommodate those who for one reason or another could not or did not wish to participate in such a long service. Perhaps the gradual anticipation of the Vigil also played a part here.

Down through history this Sunday has been given many names: *Dominica resurrectionis* (the Sunday of the [Lord's] resurrection); the *Dominica sancta* (the holy Sunday), to mention only two.

As to the name "Easter," the Venerable Bede (c. 673–735) in England wrote that the word was connected with an Anglo-Saxon spring goddess "Eostre," and yet history knows no such personage — perhaps Bede was simply misinformed or was merely making good use of his imagination in this regard. Some today believe that the remote origins of the word are to be found in the Latin phrase *hebdomada in albis* ("week in white garments"). In Germany the people misunderstood *"in albis"* as the plural of alba (dawn) and translated it as *eostarum* in Old German. At any rate, Christ is indeed the Sun who rises in the East.

Throughout history Easter Sunday became the locus for several liturgical and non-liturgical practices. For example, the Liturgy of the Word came to include the sequence *Victimae paschali laudes*, written by Wipo (d.c. 1050), a prolific hymn writer from Burgundy (or Swabia) whose verse has for the most part been lost. As to the Eucharistic celebration, various foods and the paschal lamb were blessed at its conclusion. Furthermore, during the Middle Ages various processions were connected with the Easter Sunday Mass, for example, the coming of the holy women to the empty tomb and their encounter with the angels, or the return of the apostles to Galilee.

During the seventh and eighth centuries, Rome gave special attention to the celebration of vespers. Those chanting this section of the divine office in the Lateran

Basilica went, at its conclusion, to the baptistery together with the newly baptized, and then to the Chapel of the Holy Cross. In some areas the priests were served wine after the vesper celebration, and, to express the joy of the feast, they engaged in a type of dance in the parish courtyard.

As mentioned at the beginning of this book, determining the date for the Easter Triduum was a problem in the early Church, with non-Jewish Christians being in conflict with the Jewish converts. The date of Easter remains a topic of discussion even today. The bishops attending the Second Vatican Council stated that they were not "opposed to the assignment of the Feast of Easter to a particular Sunday of the Gregorian Calendar, provided those whom it may concern, especially other Christians who are not in communion with the Apostolic See, give their assent" (*Constitution on the Sacred Liturgy*: Appendix). For example, Easter could always be celebrated on the second Sunday in April (April 8 – 14). Discussions have been held among the various churches in regard to such a change; communities having their origins in the Reformation appear to have no problem with a fixed day for Easter, and yet the Orthodox Churches are divided in their support for such a change.

Documentation

Circular Letter "Paschalis sollemnitatis"

B. Easter Day

97   Mass is to be celebrated on Easter Day with great solemnity. It is appropriate that the penitential rite on this day take the form of a sprinkling with water blessed at the Vigil, during which the antiphon *Vidi aquam*, or some other song of baptismal character should be sung. The fonts at the entrance to the church should also be filled with the same water.

98   The tradition of celebrating baptismal Vespers on Easter Day with the singing of psalms during the procession to the font should be maintained where it is still in force, and appropriately, restored.

99   The paschal candle has its proper place either by the ambo or by the altar and should be lit at least in all the more solemn liturgical celebrations of the season until Pentecost Sunday, whether at Mass, or at Morning and Evening Prayer. After the Easter season the candle should be kept with honor in the baptistry, so that in the celebration of Baptism the candles of the baptized may be lit from them. In the celebration of funerals, the paschal candle should be placed near the coffin to indicate that the death of a Christian is his own passover. The paschal candle

should not otherwise be lit nor placed in the sanctuary outside the Easter season.

Roman Missal

71 **Entrance Antiphon**   Cf. Ps 139 (138): 18, 5–6
I have risen, and I am with you still, alleluia.
You have laid your hand upon me, alleluia.
Too wonderful for me, this knowledge, alleluia, alleluia.
Or: Lk 24: 34; cf. Rev 1: 6
The Lord is truly risen, alleluia.
To him be glory and power
for all the ages of eternity, alleluia, alleluia.

The *Gloria in excelsis* (Glory to God in the highest) is said.

72 **Collect**
O God, who on this day,
through your Only Begotten Son,
have conquered death
and unlocked for us the path to eternity,
grant, we pray, that we who keep
the solemnity of the Lord's Resurrection
may, through the renewal brought by your Spirit,
rise up in the light of life.
Through our Lord Jesus Christ, your Son,
who lives and reigns with you in the unity of the Holy Spirit,
one God, for ever and ever.
[R. Amen.]

Lectionary for Mass
42

Easter Sunday A B C
The Resurrection of the Lord
The Mass of Easter Day

First Reading
We ate and drank with him after he rose from the dead.
A reading from the Acts of the Apostles   10:34a, 37–43

Peter proceeded to speak and said:
"You know what has happened all over Judea,
beginning in Galilee after the baptism
that John preached,
how God anointed Jesus of Nazareth
with the Holy Spirit and power.
He went about doing good
and healing all those oppressed by the devil,

for God was with him.
We are witnesses of all that he did
both in the country of the Jews and in Jerusalem.
They put him to death by hanging him on a tree.
This man God raised on the third day and granted that he be visible,
not to all the people, but to us,
the witnesses chosen by God in advance,
who ate and drank with him after he rose from the dead.
He commissioned us to preach to the people
and testify that he is the one appointed by God
as judge of the living and the dead.
To him all the prophets bear witness,
that everyone who believes in him
will receive forgiveness of sins through his name."

The word of the Lord.

Responsorial Psalm   Ps 118:1–2, 16–17, 22–23
R. (24) This is the day the Lord has made; let us rejoice and be glad.
or:
R. Alleluia.
Give thanks to the LORD, for he is good,
for his mercy endures forever.
Let the house of Israel say,
"His mercy endures forever."
R This is the day the Lord has made; let us rejoice and be glad.
or:
R. Alleluia.

"The right hand of the LORD has struck with power;
the right hand of the LORD is exalted.
I shall not die, but live,
and declare the works of the LORD."
R. This is the day the Lord has made; let us rejoice and be glad.
or:
R. Alleluia.

The stone which the builders rejected
has become the cornerstone.
By the LORD has this been done;
it is wonderful in our eyes.
R. This is the day the Lord has made; let us rejoice and be glad.
or:
R. Alleluia.

Second Reading
A   *Seek what is above, where Christ is.*
A reading from the Letter of Saint Paul to the Colossians   3:1–4

Brothers and sisters:
If then you were raised with Christ, seek what is above,
where Christ is seated at the right hand of God.
Think of what is above, not of what is on earth.
For you have died, and your life is hidden with Christ in God.
When Christ your life appears,
then you too will appear with him in glory.

The word of the Lord.

or

B   *Clear out the old yeast, so that you may become a fresh batch of dough.*
A reading from the first Letter of Saint Paul to the Corinthians   5:66–8

Brothers and sisters:
Do you not know that a little yeast leavens all the dough?
Clear out the old yeast,
so that you may become a fresh batch of dough,
inasmuch as you are unleavened.
For our paschal lamb, Christ, has been sacrificed.
Therefore, let us celebrate the feast,
not with the old yeast, the yeast of malice and wickedness,
but with the unleavened bread of sincerity and truth.

The word of the Lord.

Sequence   *Victimae paschali laudes*
Christians, to the Paschal Victim
Offer your thankful praises!
A Lamb the sheep redeems;
Christ, who only is sinless,
Reconciles sinners to the Father.
Death and life have contended in that combat stupendous:
The Prince of life, who died, reigns immortal.
Speak, Mary, declaring
What you saw, wayfaring.
"The tomb of Christ, who is living,
The glory of Jesus' resurrection;
Bright angels attesting,
The shroud and napkin resting.
Yes, Christ my hope is arisen;
To Galilee he goes before you."
Christ indeed from death is risen, our new life obtaining.
Have mercy, victor King, ever reigning!
Amen. Alleluia.

Alleluia   cf. 1 Cor 5:7b–8a

R. Alleluia, alleluia.

Christ, our paschal lamb, has been sacrificed;

let us then feast with joy in the Lord.

R. Alleluia, alleluia.

Gospel

At an afternoon or evening Mass, another Gospel may be read:
>   *Luke 24, 13–35*
>>   *Stay with us since it is almost evening. (see n. 46).*
The Gospel from the Easter Vigil (see n. 41) may also be read
>>   *in place of the following Gospel at any time of the day.*
>>   *He had to rise from the dead.*

A reading from the holy Gospel according to John   20:1–9

On the first day of the week,

Mary of Magdala came to the tomb early in the morning,

while it was still dark,

and saw the stone removed from the tomb.

So she ran and went to Simon Peter

and to the other disciple whom Jesus loved, and told them,

"They have taken the Lord from the tomb,

and we don't know where they put him."

So Peter and the other disciple went out and came to the tomb.

They both ran, but the other disciple ran faster than Peter

and arrived at the tomb first;

he bent down and saw the burial cloths there, but did not go in.

When Simon Peter arrived after him,

he went into the tomb and saw the burial cloths there,

and the cloth that had covered his head,

not with the burial cloths but rolled up in a separate place.

Then the other disciple also went in,

the one who had arrived at the tomb first,

and he saw and believed.

For they did not yet understand the Scripture

that he had to rise from the dead.

The Gospel of the Lord.

Roman Missal

72   The Creed is said.

However, in Easter Sunday Masses which are celebrated with a congregation, the rite of the renewal of baptismal promises may take place after the Homily, according to the text used at the Easter Vigil. In that case the Creed is omitted.

73 **Prayer over the Offerings**
Exultant with paschal gladness, O Lord,
we offer the sacrifice
by which your Church
is wondrously reborn and nourished.
Through Christ our Lord.

74 Preface I of Easter, The Paschal Mystery

When the Roman Canon is used, the proper forms of the *Communi-cantes* (In communion with those) and *Hanc igitur* (Therefore, Lord, we pray) are said.

75 **Communion Antiphon**   I Cor 5: 7–8
Christ our Passover has been sacrificed, alleluia;
therefore let us keep the feast with the unleavened bread
of purity and truth, alleluia, alleluia.

76 **Prayer after Communion**
Look upon your Church, O God,
with unfailing love and favor,
so that, renewed by the paschal mysteries,
she may come to the glory of the resurrection.
Through Christ our Lord.

77 To impart the blessing at the end of Mass, the Priest may appropriately use the formula of Solemn Blessing for the Mass of the Easter Vigil.

78 For the dismissal of the people, there is sung (as above no. 69) or said:
Go forth, the Mass is ended, alleluia, alleluia.
Or:
Go in peace, alleluia, alleluia.
R. Thanks be to God, alleluia, alleluia.

Constitution on the Sacred Liturgy: Appendix.
On Revision of the Calendar

131 The Second Vatican Ecumenical Council recognizes the importance of the wishes expressed by many on assigning the feast of Easter to a fixed Sunday and on an unchanging calendar and has considered the effects that could result from the introduction of a new calendar. Accordingly the Council issues the following declaration:

1 The Council is not opposed to the assignment of the feast of Easter to a particular Sunday of the Gregorian Calendar, provided those

whom it may concern, especially other Christians who are not in communion with the Apostolic See, give their assent.

2 The Council likewise declares that it does not oppose measures designed to introduce a perpetual calendar into civil society.

Among the various systems being suggested to establish a perpetual calendar and to introduce into civil life, only those systems are acceptable to the Church that retain and safeguard a seven-day week with Sunday and introduce no days outside the week, so that the present sequence of weeks is left intact, unless the most serious reasons arise. Concerning these the Apostolic See will make its own judgment.

Decree "Orientalium Ecclesiarum" on the Eastern Catholic Churches

20 Until attainment of the desired agreement among all Christians on a common date for the celebration of Easter, it is left to patriarchs or the highest territorial ecclesiastical authorities, in order to promote unity among Christians of the same region or nation, to concur, with unanimous consent and after consultation of all interested parties, on celebrating Easter on the same Sunday.

Reflection

"How beautiful is the paschal celebration. Beautiful too is the present assembly. The mysteries contain so much that is both old and new. . . . It is not just those on earth who rejoice but also the powers above who join in our activities and celebrate with us because of the resurrection of Christ. For now the angels join in the feast, and the hosts of archangels celebrate the king of heaven, Christ our God received as victor returned from earth to heaven. The choirs of saints keep festival too: they proclaim Christ risen before the dawn (Ps 110:3). The earth celebrates the feast . . . the sea celebrates . . . let every person celebrate, born again of water and the Holy Spirit" (Proclus of Constantinople *[d. 446]*).

Suggested Questions for Discussion

1 Given the amount of work involved in the Thursday, Friday, and Vigil liturgies, what can be done so that the Easter Sunday celebration not appear as anticlimactic?

2 Should the adults who were initiated during the Vigil be encouraged to return for the Easter Sunday celebration?

3   What does the sequence add to today's celebration. Should the piece be sung or recited?

4   Some parishes baptize on Easter Sunday those infants who could not be baptized during the Vigil. Good idea or not?

5   Is it a good idea to celebrate first communions on Easter Sunday?

6   How can a parish establish a tradition of celebrating evening prayer on Easter Sunday?

Bibliography

• Hollerweger, Hans. "Is Easter Sunday Being Neglected? Two Suggestions." In *Celebrating the Easter Vigil*, ed. Rupert Berger and Hans Hollerweger, tr. Matthew J. O'Connell. New York: Pueblo Publishing Company, 1983. 138-141.

18033904R00105

Made in the USA
Charleston, SC
12 March 2013